HEART STORMING

The Way to a Purposeful Life

FATHER PAUL KEENAN

Contemporary Books

Chicago   New York   San Francisco   Lisbon   London   Madrid   Mexico City
Milan   New Delhi   San Juan   Seoul   Singapore   Sydney   Toronto

Library of Congress Cataloging-in-Publication Data

Keenan, Paul.
    Heartstorming : the way to a purposeful life / Paul Keenan.
        p.   cm.
    Includes bibliographical references and index.
    ISBN 0-8092-9478-8
    1. Christian life—Catholic authors.   2. Spiritual life—Catholic
Church.   I. Title.

    BX2350.2.K4267   2001
    248.4'82—dc21   2001017065

Contemporary Books
A Division of The McGraw·Hill Companies

1 2 3 4 5 6 7 8 9 0   LBM/LBM   0 9 8 7 6 5 4 3 2 1

ISBN 0-8092-9478-8

This book was set in Bembo
Printed and bound by Lake Book Manufacturing
Interior design by Jeanette Wojtyla

In loving memory of Ned Giordano,
who told us all to "go safe,"
and who, by the gift of his friendship,
made it possible for us to do so.

Contents

PART III
HEARTSTORMING IN EVERYDAY LIFE

Acknowledgments

As always, I am deeply grateful to Denise Marcil, my literary agent. Though she prefers to remain in the shadows of her authors, her undying support for them simply must be brought to light. I would like to extend my gratitude to John Nolan, Judith McCarthy, Michelle Pezzutti, Cori Spragg, and all the wonderful people at Contemporary Books whose support, encouragement, and friendship have gone far beyond the call of duty. To the Archdiocese of New York—most especially to Edward Cardinal Egan and Joseph Zwilling, director of the Office of Communications, who have given me green lights and warm support in my various endeavors. To the wonderful people at WABC and WOR Radio, who have allowed me to broadcast on their airwaves. There are so many friends, colleagues, and benefactors who deserve thanks. You cannot all be named here, lest this

xii   *Acknowledgments*

acknowledgment become a book in itself, but you know that you have my undying gratitude and love and an everlasting remembrance in my prayers. To Susan Zappo, whose supportive presence gives me hope and encouragement, especially in the tough times. To my cats Teddy, Midnight, and Lionel, with thanks for daily strength and love, as we continue to remember our beloved Flicka. And to all of you, dear readers, who are kind enough to share your time and space with me. Happy journeys, and may your hearts be filled with the joy of God's abundant love.

PART I

WHAT IS
*H*EARTSTORMING?

CHAPTER ONE

Like a Ship on a Stormy Sea

"The human heart," wrote Martin Luther, "is like a ship on a stormy sea driven about by winds blowing from all four corners of heaven." What a remarkably accurate description of the part of ourselves we call the *heart*. It's a difficult word to define because it is so intimate to us. Defining it is like trying to define our own skin. "Well, it's, you know, it's like, well, my feelings," someone said to me not long ago when I asked him what his heart was. The Hebrews had it right when they used the word *leb* to express the idea of the heart. It derives from words meaning "agitated motion." Often enough, that is how we experience our heart. Just as our physical heart ebbs and flows, pumping with the rush of blood, so does our emotional heart rise and fall with the push and pull of our feelings. Just as the doctor takes our blood pressure with its systole and diastole, so do we frequently measure the highs and lows of our heart, the rise and fall of our emotions.

We often describe the heart as a treasure chest containing inner riches. In the Bible, St. Luke tells us that Mary, the mother of Jesus, "treasured in her heart" the strange and wonderful things that had been happening to her since the conception of her son, Jesus. The heart is indeed like a treasure chest in which many things are stored—some joyful, some tragic.

The heart can be broken. "Had we never lov'd sae kindly / Had we never lov'd sae blindly, / Never met—or never parted— / We had ne'er been broken-hearted." Robert Burns was right. The heart, like a precious ceramic vase or jewel box, contains the treasured memories of a lifetime and beyond. When it is broken, we might feel that it may never be put back together again.

The heart, though in ways different from the brain, is a thinker. Shakespeare's quip that "to say the truth, reason and love keep little company together now-a-days" rings as true in twenty-first-century America is it did in Elizabethan England. We're not used to the heart thinking; we have enough trouble thinking with our brain. Nonetheless, the heart has a logic of its own, as Blaise Pascal told us: "The heart has its reasons which reason knows not of." When I was in graduate studies in philosophy, I had the privilege of studying under Dr. Elizabeth Kraus, a brilliant scholar whose classes were full of heart. During those years, Liz taught us about her philosophy of love. "Love," she told us, "is thought before it hardens."

What a magnificent description of love, and what it tells us about the heart! Before we can conceptualize anything, we need to take it in though our *senses*. The word means "feeling"—our senses are our way of feeling out our world. Beyond sight, taste, hearing, touch, and smell, however, there is a feeling-association that accompanies our senses. One night, after going for a walk, I came home to find half a dozen fire trucks lined up outside the rectory in which I was living. I saw the red trucks and their flashing lights and heard their sirens. But along with all of that, I felt a tremendous sense of danger, of fear and panic, in the pit of my stomach. Then I was able to conceptualize what was going on. The logic of the heart told me that there was danger before my mind knew it was so. Fortunately, no one was injured, and the only damage was from the smoke. Yet a bit of that fear recurs whenever I see or hear a fire truck. It seems to go along with the concept.

The heart is a precious vase that holds the impressions and feelings that are so close to us and that are so much a part of our knowledge of the world. As Martin Luther said, and as the Hebrew language attested before him, the heart is often full of agitation. We experience things all the time, each of which brings with it feelings and impressions of pleasure or pain, joy or sorrow, calm or anger, fear or confidence. All of those feelings can be swirling around inside of us at the same time and color our view of life.

∞

I learned a lot about the heart's ability to color our world when, as a young priest, I was assigned as a hospital chaplain for a brief period after ordination. One of my chief duties was to visit patients in the hospital. That experience gave me some powerful lessons as to how the heart affects our view of life.

I noticed this especially in the ways I would be greeted by the patients. Most of the time, they would greet me warmly and with open hearts. Early on, I remember visiting a gentleman whose leg had become so badly infected that he was in danger of needing it amputated. He spoke with me very openly and honestly, sharing his fears with me as though he were talking to a brother or a close friend. At the end of our conversation, he asked me if I would pray for him. I placed my hand very gently on his leg, and he and I prayed together. Shortly afterward, I noticed that he had been discharged from the hospital. I wondered if our prayers had been answered.

A few weeks later, when I walked into a room, there was my friend back again. But this time, his infected leg was gone. He had undergone the surgery after all. I was embarrassed;

but, to my amazement, he showed no resentment toward God or toward me. On the contrary, he radiated peace.

As a young and inexperienced priest, I almost wanted to apologize to the man. I felt like a failure, and wondered why God had not allowed me to heal him. It was years later that I realized how much this patient had taught me about having an accepting heart. I still do not understand why he was not healed *as we had asked*. The difference between my heart and his heart was that his remained open and accepting in the face of disappointment, while mine did not. I was too busy attaching ego to my prayers and reacting self-centeredly because my prayers "didn't work." Once I realized that, my heart was ready to let in a new insight. Perhaps the prayer we had said together had healed his heart, though not his leg, and enabled him to bask in that peaceful acceptance. Once I saw that—years later, mind you—my heart was healed as well.

Not all the hearts I encountered during my hospital tenure were as open as that man's was. When the heart is closed and full of rancor, it becomes difficult to gain entry to it. Some patients thought that the priest walking into their room was a sure sign that they were about to die. I remember walking into the room of an elderly woman who, the minute she saw me, sat bolt upright and screamed at the top of her voice for me to get out. Today, I might try to cajole her or try to break down the barrier in some other way. But then, I was a scared young priest, and all I could think of was what Jesus told his disciples, "Shake the dust of the town from your feet"

(Matthew 10:14). I am ashamed to say, I fled. Her heart was frightened and so was mine, and we perceived one another as threats. We both lost an opportunity for grace.

∞

Is the heart the same as the soul? Is there a distinction between the two? We often use the words interchangeably, and the dictionary does not distinguish all that clearly between them. I believe that they are separate faculties that interact deeply with one another. The soul is the fundamental principle of life. The heart is the seat of the feelings and impressions. The soul provides a home for the tumultuous and often confusing impressions that the heart contains, and attempts to bring them to peace by holding them up to eternal values, such as truth, beauty, hope, and love.

I see the heart as a conduit to the soul. It holds together in one place all of our feelings and impressions. It is the soul that brings us beyond the limited perspective that feelings and impressions give us, and instead reveals an external perspective. By putting them in touch with eternity, it cleanses and purifies them by taking what is truly lasting in them and holding it.

The heart and the soul are partners. The heart gathers our feelings as a hen gathers her chicks. The soul takes the confused mixture of the things our heart holds and tries to make sense of them—not by conceptualizing them, as the mind does, but in its own unique way, by touching them with ultimate meaning and reality. The heart reaches to the soul for a lifeline, a sense of purpose. The soul, in turn, reaches to the heart for fulfillment. They long for each other and are incomplete without each other. They are, in that sense, the perfect prototype of lovers.

That sounds very romantic; but as anyone knows who has ever loved, lovers have a propensity to fight. Not always or every day, but sometimes, to be sure.

The heart can become frustrated with the soul in many ways. Sometimes the heart longs for some sense of ultimacy. It is so mixed-up and confused, full of so many things, and it longs for some meaning to it all. Just when the heart is feeling that kind of pressing urgency, the soul may decide to take its time, to play among its ideals, to mull things over. That can drive the heart crazy, make it frustrated. It can also make it want to give up on the possibility of finding meaning.

That can happen in times of depression. In fact, depression is sometimes part of a long stretch of waiting and the feeling of endlessness that can weigh so heavily upon us during such stretches. In mid-life, it is not unusual to experience lengthy periods of wondering whether life has any real value. Work days become tedious and lackluster. Leisure time becomes filled with groups, classes, bars and restaurants, shopping, nonstop television programs, and even prayer groups—all of which create the same, dull, monotonous, flat sensation after a while. "How come there are a hundred channels on our cable system and nothing good on television?" we cry. Another familiar complaint: "I've read all of the books on relationships, joined singles groups, gone on lots of dates. How come there's nobody out there for me?" Again: "I've spent my whole life being a good person. I've been decent and honest, fair to others, giving, and caring. Why am I having this string of bad luck?" Or this: "All my life I've prayed, gone to church, and believed in God. Why does it seem that I'm being punished?"

At just these moments, when these feelings and the questions that accompany them pressure us, we want immediate answers. After all, our needs and our questions seem very clear. We want concrete direction, and it seems that we are never going to find it. We get mad at ourselves, at our spouses, at our boss, at life, and often at God.

What we don't realize, when our souls seem to be too slow for our minds and our hearts, is that the soul always goes for depth, not for speed. That can drive us crazy. We have needs, questions, places to go, and only a short amount of time.

I remember well the early years of my radio program "As You Think." I was engaged in a long struggle to raise the funds that were needed to keep the program on the air. It was a day-to-day, week-to-week struggle to find sponsors and donors who would come up with each week's check to pay the station. My heart was always frustrated and on edge. I read books on prosperity. I cold-called sponsors until I was blue. I tried various fund-raising ventures, all of which raised less money than I'd hoped for. I thought I had surrendered everything into the hands of God. Meanwhile, I was watching other ministries succeed beyond all telling. I became increasingly frustrated with myself, with God, and with the situation. Granted, we always managed to stay on the air, but why couldn't we be as successful as the others, more than just keeping our head above water?

That's what happens when the heart and mind are overwhelmed and come to believe that the soul is nowhere to be found. Besides being common, this rift between heart and soul is the fundamental alienation that a human being can experience. It is searing, because it represents the ultimate disappointment, the feeling that somehow God is not blessing *our* work while he is blessing everyone else's abundantly.

Here is where *heartstorming* comes in. Heartstorming is a process by which we look seriously and directly at our feelings about our situation, to see what our heart is telling us. Then we allow the mind to work on the feelings and impressions, to see if there are any conclusions we can draw or solutions we can reach. Finally, we cross the threshold into the realm of soul, to "see life steadily and see it whole," as poet Matthew Arnold said. In the realm of soul, we tend to get answers quite different from those of the feeling heart and the reasoning mind. In the soul, we experience life without urgency, without conditions, without limits, and with enormous breadth of possibility, perspective, and depth. Lately,

I've noticed that in the city I feel cramped and confined, while out in the country I feel refreshed, renewed, and energized. Life just seems bigger and broader out there. A friend who lives in the country but commutes to and from the city tells me that there is a certain point on the drive at which she knows she is in the country again. She can feel herself expanding. Similarly, when we enter the realm of soul, we find our sights expanding and we can breathe again.

I speak of *heartstorming* as opposed to *brainstorming* or *soulstorming* (turning inward to receive the soul's guidance), because heartstorming embraces the full human person in a way that the others do not. If I'm stuck and brainstorm about it, I end up (I hope) with lots of ideas; but on what basis do I separate the ideas and decide what to do? Perhaps I pick the idea that comes to mind most often. Perhaps I choose the course of action that is the easiest, or the most difficult. Perhaps I choose the one everybody else likes, even though I hate it.

Or perhaps, instead of brainstorming, I go within to the depths of my soul to soulstorm. A friend once told me, "The summer before I was to enter the seminary, I met the girl of my dreams and fell head over heels in love. I talked to my parish priest, who advised me to go away on retreat and pray to know God's will. I prayed and meditated, went for long walks, sat for hours in chapel, and did a lot of spiritual reading. By the end of the weekend, I was more confused than

ever. It seemed that God could be calling me in both directions. I was a mess." Often when the heart is torn, the soul,
whose purpose is to put us in touch with God, has a hard
time getting through.

In making life decisions, it is necessary to consult the heart
as well as the mind and the soul. Brainstorming and soul-
storming are just too abstract to motivate us to action.

Marjorie loved her large suburban house and adored her
husband and teenage son and daughter. Her life was wonderful, her marriage solid. Yet she wondered why she wasn't
happy. She read every self-help book in sight, took Italian
classes, learned to do topiary. Mornings, when she was alone,
she would sit and meditate by the pool. Yet she felt empty
inside. Like a snowball gathering momentum, the emptiness
grew until she thought she couldn't stand it any longer. *What
was left?* she asked herself. She had tried ideas, activities, and
soul-searching. Something should have worked by now. Or
was life an emotional dead end?

Like most of us at some point in our lives, Marjorie fed
her mind and soul in her search for happiness. What she
needed to do was to feed her heart. What her heart needed
most of all was for her to listen to it, simply listen. Once she
agreed to listen, her heart would show her how to make the
most of what her mind and her soul had to offer.

Marjorie had "been there and done that" in terms of self-
help and inspiration, and still couldn't get going. Heart-

storming is a much more tangible and concrete way to get off the dime.

Heartstorming touches us at our center, our core (a word that, as we shall see, derives from the Latin word for "heart"). Instead of examining our ideas or our ideals, heartstorming takes us directly to the depths of our hearts. As we examine what is in our hearts, we are amazed to discover both the ideas and the ideals that we live by. For example, if I am heartbroken over the death of a loved one, I may discover in my mind the idea that life is too difficult for me to go on, and also discover in my soul the beauty and love that can coexist with deep suffering. Both of these have an impact on the heart. The former might make the heart sad (discouraged, dis-heartened, we say), while the latter might inspire it (en-courage).

The true purpose of heartstorming is to give us passion with balance. The energy of passion is twofold: toward (what I'll call) impassionment and toward compassion.

Impassionment means passion from within ourselves. Heartstorming brings us right inside our feelings and lets us know what drives us. A friend who had undergone a number of miscarriages and abortions had no idea of her feelings about them. One day, while reading a newspaper article about the discovery of the dead body of a baby, she began to weep uncontrollably and discovered deep-seated feelings of grief and guilt. As she dealt with these feelings with the help of a kind counselor, the feelings melded into a desire to help other women in similar situations. Since then, her passion has been befriending thousands of women who have lost babies before birth.

The beauty of impassionment is that it can couple with *compassion*. My friend's impassionment yielded a compassion—a heartfelt understanding of others like herself. Compassion brings passion to the level of community and draws the energies of one's heart beyond itself.

Paradoxically, then, heartstorming takes us deep within ourselves, and at the same time draws us into the hearts of others.

This book will show you how to heartstorm. It may lead you to discover a passion, even a degree of *com*passion that you never knew before.

In *Heartstorming*, I will take you through the process of coming to inner balance and peace. It is a process that I went through myself, and the midsection of the book will elucidate the felt images and memories that enabled me to rekindle my heart, which had shown signs of losing its joy in life. I will also tell the stories of others who have taken a similar path to inner peace. Because each person is so different, no two people's heartstorming processes will be quite the same; yet amazingly, when people hear the heartstorming stories of others, they somehow feel like kindred spirits.

The heartstorming process is so accessible to people. One need not undergo an arduous pilgrimage, enter a ten-step program, or follow a rigorous diet. All that heartstorming requires is a little silence, a pen and a few sheets of paper, and a few examples or stories to prime the heart. Once the heart begins to flow, the soul and the mind can direct the heart's feelings toward the steadiness it seeks.

I discovered my own process of heartstorming at a time in my life when everything on the outside was going wonderfully, but inside I felt as though the bloom had fallen from the rose. I had published two books and was working on a third. I was hosting two very successful radio programs and doing some national radio commentary. I was living and assisting in a wonderful parish. But my heart felt like somebody had poured cement on it and paved it over. I found myself going through the motions of a busy schedule. With a little brainstorming I thought of all sorts of options, from getting a new assignment to taking a vacation—but all of the options felt like something else to do. I then did some soul-storming, praying and meditating, petitioning God for an answer—but nothing much happened.

It finally dawned on me that what I needed was to jump-start my heart. I realized that it wasn't for lack of ideas or prayers that I was feeling so blah—it was for lack of a fire in my heart. A line from Robert Louis Stevenson kept hitting me: "The world is so full of a number of things. I'm sure we should all be as happy as kings." I wondered why my heart didn't feel full. I began to think about my heart and about some of the words that relate to the heart, words like *courage* and *core*. Memories of wonderful times and sad times came into play, along with the lyrics of songs I loved about the heart, such as "Happy Heart" and "Dear Heart." A childhood devotion to the Sacred Heart of Jesus helped me to uncover in my heart some people whose hearts were sacred to me.

Oddly enough, at this time several very dear friends died, and I found myself heartstorming about my loss of them. All in all, I found myself coming alive again in my heart, experiencing joy and peace in the realization that some feelings I had thought were gone forever were really everlasting—which, I recalled, is what the soul shows us when it is connected to the heart. My mind became creative again, and I was able to find ways to use my time differently. I had discovered a process of heartstorming that brought my soul and my mind into play. I began to experience a passion for life again.

Looking back, I see that my heartstorming process put me in touch with three questions that can guide us all as we heartstorm. The questions are:

1. What matters? (What do I feel in my heart?)

2. What do I believe in? (What does my mind tell me about what I feel?)

3. What brings me joy and peace? (What are the ideals and inspirations of my soul?)

Heartstorming espouses a fundamental belief that life really matters and that something besides our own self-interest matters. That belief must be paramount if we are to live fully and effectively.

As we pursue these questions, we find ourselves growing in understanding of what matters to us. We begin to discover our passion. The beauty of including the soul and the mind in the process is that they tend to draw us to interests beyond ourselves. The mind draws us to overriding beliefs, and the soul draws us to ideals and values. But rather than diminishing the heart by taking it out of its focus on itself, the process actually expands the heart by getting it excited about what is important for others and for the world at large. I found that heartstorming helped me get out of myself and my "blahs" and fall in love with life again. Impassionment and compassion go hand in hand.

That's what happened to the friend I mentioned who, out of her own heartbreaking losses, helps women who have lost children through abortion, stillbirth, and miscarriage. She understands their pain firsthand, and helping them is her passion now. A middle-aged man, devastated by the painful death of his wife from cancer, found himself reaching out to couples whose marriages needed help, and now spends countless happy hours with them. Having been deeply in love with his wife, he understands what married people feel. When we find our passion, we find we can have compassion for others, and we are often surprised to discover how much joy we experience in being there for them.

With all of the hopes people have expressed for the new millennium, heartstorming is a process whose time has come. From the twentieth century we bring with us an explosion of information and a wealth of soulfulness, but a lot of puzzlement about our hearts. Far and away, most of the questions I am asked on my talk radio programs are from people who want to understand life and do what is right, but don't understand why they feel so lost and confused. "I've been driving around all evening," a caller once told me, "and I happened to tune in, and I felt that you were talking to me. I couldn't wait to get home and call you." I hear this a lot from listeners and from readers of my books; and like so many other callers, this one came to me brokenhearted and confused. But also a little angry: when we don't listen to our hearts, our minds, and our souls, all three resent it very much. Without each other, they are incomplete and frustrated, and so are we. It's why so much rage and violence exist in our homes and in our schools these days.

Heartstorming teaches us how to find peace and balance in a way that lasts, because it involves the heart with the mind and the soul, as it was designed to be. As you follow my heartstorming, you will begin to do your own. You'll discover what matters to you, what you believe about yourself and life, and what your values are. You will be amazed at how much you will learn, and how alive you will come to feel.

The power of the heart is simply amazing.

∞

Chapters 2 through 22 will take you through the various aspects of my own heartstorming. You will certainly pick different subjects for your process than I did for mine. Mine came from phrases and song lyrics, from my fascination with words, from things I normally associate with the heart, from memories of people I have loved, and from life problems. You can heartstorm about anything. The key is to come alive to your heart, to give its moods and feelings expression and content and, finally, meaning and soul. Then you go back to your world renewed and inspired, perhaps even feeling a little better for a broadened perspective.

There is no magical number of topics to heartstorm about. For present purposes, I wanted to provide enough examples so that you would have a good feel for how to do it yourself. It didn't seem fair to whet your whistle and then leave you hanging.

Each chapter has three sections. The first section discusses or describes the particular topic from the point of view of the heart. Then the mind takes over in the second section and tries to give definition to the heart's contribution to the topic and, where appropriate, a reasonable line of solution to the problem at hand. The third section takes you into the soul, where you will encounter grace and mystery and a whole new way of looking at things. You'll notice that the soul's way of resolving things is often different from the mind's, though it builds upon it. You will find, as you move through each chapter, that you are using more and more of your human capacities, that you are bringing richer fare to the table of life. You will find yourself more inclined to feast on life rather than to be eaten alive by it.

Heartstorming is intended to help you to get more out of life, to bring more of yourself to your life. Its purposes are not pragmatic, yet at the end we shall find that we have learned some very practical wisdom for our lives. Some people might use it as a way of expanding their vision and expression. Fiction writers whose bread and butter is looking at the same thing from different viewpoints will find the exercise of looking at something in three different ways refreshing and helpful in plot development. Poets looking for unique and spirited ways to express a feeling or idea will find at least three whole clusters of feelings, thoughts, and images arising from each heartstorming reflection. The same is true of musicians, artists, dancers, and other participants in the arts.

Heartstorming will probably not put food on your table, but businesspeople at all levels—management, sales, human resources, product distribution, and so on—will find it help-ing them to look at ordinary things from refreshingly new, even spiritual, points of view. The trend toward bringing spirituality into business finds a unique and heretofore untapped dimension in *Heartstorming*. People in the caring professions, tired from long hours of dedicated service, will find here a simple and effective way of reflection that will open up to them new sources of energy and new resources for their lives and work. People with the blahs, people in cri-sis, people stuck in life—all will find in *Heartstorming* ways to come alive again.

Are you ready to join with me in an adventure that will change your life?

PART II

HEARTSTORMING

Watching the Heart, Mind, and Soul
Work Together

CHAPTER TWO

A Garden in Your Heart

Gardens have always played an important role in my life. When I was a young child, my mother developed a daily ritual of taking me for an afternoon visit to the park. I recall seeing row after row of beautiful roses, tulips, daffodils. I watched the sun illuminating their gorgeous colors and the rain refreshing their petals and roots with its gentle moisture. Those early memories of flowers are also my first impressions of primary colors. The vivid reds and yellows, the lush green of the grass and blue of the sky, told me early on that life was vivid, joyous, and alive.

At a time when I was opening up to life myself, trying out a new body, I saw the flowers as friends that supported my quest for life. As I touched their velvet petals, inhaled their perfume, and took in their rich and varied hues, I felt secure in my exploration of life. Gardens made my new world a friendly place. I could visit my floral friends every day; and when I did, they warmed my soul, entertained it, and made me happy. To this day, when I visit a botanical garden or see one in a photo, I feel an aliveness that I know to be the legacy of those childhood flowers.

Later in life, I learned that there is an energy that comes up from the earth that heals and centers us. As a child, I knew very little of such things, but I now realize that this is what I was experiencing. The gardens of my infancy helped me to feel safe and secure. Visiting them was like going to the home of a beloved aunt whose presence and familiar smell makes you feel that the world is safe.

In those infant days, gardens were something I went to visit. Home was a three-room apartment on the third floor of a house. Knowing my mother, I'm sure there must have been flowers in the house, but I don't recall any. I remember Peter, our canary; a sofa; and my father's old wooden tube radio (not so antique in those days). I watched with excitement as the tubes glowed and the speaker crackled. I remember my father's easy chair—I have his footstool in my living room today. I remember the huge electric stove that I was forbidden to touch. But I don't remember flowers. My earliest memories of flowers are that they were friends to visit in gardens, not friends to have at home.

Wait—there was one exception, an important one. My Grandmother Keenan was an artist, a painter. I am told she was a lovely woman, but she died when I was two and I truly don't remember her. What I do remember are her paintings—always of flowers and vases, still lifes, many of which decorated our home. I was about two or three when my mother took me to the gardens, and any hint I had of gardens at home was due entirely to my grandmother's paintings.

All of that changed when my parents bought their first house, a five-room bungalow with a front yard and a back yard spacious enough for gardens. Flower gardens in the front and all around the sides of the house. A vegetable garden— a true miracle—in the back. Gardens suddenly became a part of life at home.

And what a part of life they were! As if by magic, my parents planted a marvelous vegetable garden replete with corn, tomatoes, and, as I recall, cucumbers, although that seems to me a little far-fetched. "There's nothing like home-grown tomatoes," my father would say, and he was right. Out of the garden and onto our plates came the plumpest, ripest, juiciest tomatoes you ever saw. The ears of corn my parents produced in their garden were out of this world. My friends and I loved to play among the stalks, where we felt as though we were surrounded by a huge forest. We were much smaller in those days, of course, and could easily play tag, I-Spy, and Blindman's Bluff there. Best of all, we were at home, literally in our own back yard. The garden provided us ample space to play and imagine.

If my parents' vegetable gardens were wonderful, their flower gardens were truly a sight to behold. Trellises covered with American Beauty roses adorned our front door. The gardens all around the immediate edge of the house provided not only beauty, but also a rich supply of new words to learn: snapdragons, marigolds, peonies, bachelor's buttons. I loved to hold the snapdragons between my thumb and forefinger and make them snap! I don't recall that we had jack-in-the-pulpit in our garden, but I remember seeing them elsewhere and being utterly fascinated. In retrospect, perhaps that fascination foretold my future career!

In later years and in other houses, the most memorable smell from our back yard would be that of barbecue. But in those days, the bouquet that wafted from our garden was deliciously floral. It was a true bouquet—not in the sense of quantity, but in the sense of quality. To us, a bouquet is a dozen or so flowers bundled together in a decorative way—a "bouquet of flowers," we say.

In truth, the essence of a bouquet has nothing to do with the number of flowers or their arrangement. In the truest sense, a bouquet is a fragrance, the sweet and precious aroma a garden of flowers presents. "Presents" is right; the flowers give us a present, the gift of their fragrance. Walk through a garden of roses, hibiscus, or sweet alyssum, and you'll know what I mean.

The word *bouquet* in its purest sense is not lost on those who love wine. Here the bouquet is noticed by the tongue as much as by the nose. A Merlot's bouquet is denser than that of a Pinot Grigio, and that of a Chablis is more delicate than that of a Burgundy. Wine connoisseurs take it even further, distinguishing by year and village. The bouquet of wines and of flowers is a precious gift that touches and elevates the soul.

When we moved to other houses, I know my parents had flower gardens—never again vegetable gardens, as I recall. None of them held for me the magic of those earlier home gardens of my childhood. As an adult I returned to public gardens, to discover they had lost none of their ability to tease and inspire my soul. Teaching in Kansas City, I would often walk to Jacob Loose Park, just minutes away from Rockhurst University and not far at all from the Country Club Plaza. Studying theology in Berkeley, California, I would walk ten minutes to a nearby rose garden and learn theology there. In graduate school, the magic of the New York Botanical Gardens helped me to focus during a disorienting time in my life.

∞

In the New Testament, Jesus responds to a question as to why he teaches in parables, stories taken from daily life to illustrate a point. He responds by saying, "so that seeing they may not see, and hearing they may not understand." That sounds like a funny thing for a teacher to say. Teachers are supposed to want their students to grasp the material—to learn and to understand, right? What was Jesus thinking? A wise teacher, he wanted his lessons not to be memorized and learned (and forgotten) quickly. He knew that lessons learned gradually and with depth were the ones that would be most important. They would truly touch the *heart*. The nature of the truths that Jesus was teaching was such that it took a while to "get" them. Jesus knew that if the disciples took their time and mulled over the parables, they would eventually grasp what he was teaching, not only in their minds but also—more important—in their hearts.

That's how it was with me and gardens. For a good five decades of my life, I had visited gardens, played in them, and loved them without ever arriving at the great lesson that they were birthing in my heart. One morning, I was reading an E-mail from my friend Peggy Rouse, herself a gardener. Peggy's message that morning happened to contain the phrase "a garden in your heart."

It occurred to me that indeed my heart was like a garden, in many different ways. Just as the gardens of my life had various flowers and vegetables, each of which created an aspect of life, so my heart was full of various feelings and impressions, each of which created life in various shades and tones.

Reflecting on this, I realized how often we tend to ignore, overlook, or even stifle the diverse flowers in the garden of our heart. If instead we would allow all of the flowers—the good and the bad, the painful and the pleasant, the dull and the exciting—to have their due, we would find ourselves less emotionally stifled and living richer emotional lives.

What do I mean by this? Here's an example. Recently, I was having one of my radio phone chats with Thomas Moore on my program "As You Think." We were discussing his insightful book *Original Self*, and we began to talk about the feeling of sadness. Sadness is something that we usually consider undesirable, even bad. We are constantly telling each other, "Cheer up" and "Don't be sad." We beat up on ourselves when we are feeling down or morose. Yet there is an appropriateness to a time of sadness. Sadness contributes a variety of wonderful and positive things to our emotional life, if only we let it. My sadness at being separated from someone I love gives rise to the virtue of honor and pays tribute to the value of our relationship in my life. Sadness can also herald the need for a change. Perhaps I feel sad because I have been somehow mistreating people around me, and my downheartedness is telling me that there's something wrong with what I have been doing. Or maybe I'm sad because I feel my life is chronically unfulfilling—my sadness is urging me to look in new directions. More and more I hear stories of cancer survivors whose emotional devastation over their illness led them to create or to join groups or undertake activities that helped them and others to find new purpose in their lives. One woman I recently read about organizes cross-country bike trips for breast cancer survivors like herself. What an inventive way of telling sadness to hit the road!

There is nothing inherently wrong with being sad. Sadness is a flower in the garden of the heart, and it needs to be cared for and nurtured. Generally we do one of two things with sadness—ignore it or kill it. To ignore sadness usually results in turning it into a weed and letting it take over our garden. We attempt to eat it away, or drink it away, or drive it away, or work it away, or spend it away. Yet we are still sad, and we wonder why. Alternatively, we try to kill sadness, sometimes with a firm determination to "be positive." I am a firm believer in affirmations, but not when they are used to silence our sadness by pretending we are happy, happy, happy. Sadness is a gift, and we do the heart a favor when we give it its proper place in the garden of the heart.

One of the reasons, I think, that we are uneasy with sadness is that so often we confuse it with depression. People commonly describe themselves as depressed when they are merely sad. Clinical depression has an edge of sadness to it, but ordinary sadness does not shut us down emotionally and physically the way depression does. Clinical depression, like sadness, can prove to be a rich source of new life when properly addressed. But being sad is not the same as being clinically depressed. We would certainly do well not to rush for medications to take our sadness away. Sadness has a place in the garden, and has much to give us.

Sadness is only one example of the feelings we so often run from because we consider them negative or shameful. I could also speak of anger, fear, envy, and so on. They, too, are flowers in our heart's garden. They have color and texture and a certain beauty to contribute to our lives. We must not ignore them, lest they overrun the garden. But we must not stifle them. Each flower has its proper place.

Worry is another of those flowers, and it is common enough to warrant a special mention. Like sadness, worry is something we often try to eliminate from the garden of our heart. It is typically regarded as a bad thing, but I think that is perhaps because we do not listen to our worries soon enough. Like sadness, unattended worrying can take over the heart and consume it. However, if we attend to our worrying soon enough, we can find that it gives us some sound advice. In the normal course of events, when worry is listened to, it goes away.

Not all worry is excessive. Worrying often helps us to deal with legitimate issues. Worrying when loved ones are sick can remind us to pray for them or even to get them treatment if they are not taking action themselves. Worrying about our children motivates us to be conscientious about their welfare and safety. Worrying is good and beneficial when it spurs us to effective action.

OK, but what about worry that gets out of control, the kind that turns us into "worrywarts"? When worry sends us

into a tailspin, it is often enough a sign of an underlying inse-
curity and unrest that we would do well to take a look at.
Worry of this kind is a sign that we do not feel safe in the
world. The world appears to be out to get us, and we feel that
we must be constantly be on guard. As we shall see momentarily, there is a soulful response to these worries; but for the
mind's response the best thing is to examine the beliefs that
are causing the worry. *Do I really believe that there is not enough
health or money or time for me to do what I need to do? Do I really
believe that I am not gifted enough to be successful? Do I believe
that I am apparently left out while others have a good life? Do I
believe that the world is unfriendly?*

Perhaps the answer to all of the above is "yes." That's OK.
The point is to understand and identify those beliefs. Doing
this is very healthy. When we are overwhelmed by life we
can easily lose touch with what we are thinking. That's the
power of panic—it robs us of our capacity to think. When
we take time to examine what we believe about our situation,
then we take the worry and panic out of its perpetual motion
and give ourselves the opportunity to evaluate our feelings.

It is important to note that at this point we are simply
looking to identify our beliefs about life. Just doing that can
help prevent nagging worry. Identifying our beliefs gives us
a couple of advantages. First, it helps us to see that there is a
certain reasonableness about our worrying—to realize that
even if we don't like the beliefs we discover, at least it is not

entirely unreasonable to have them. Before, all we could do was worry; now, at least we know why we are worrying.

This leads to the second advantage to identifying our beliefs—doing so gives us an opportunity to decide which of those beliefs, if any, we want to keep, and which, if any, we want to change. There may be plenty of reasons for thinking that the world is unfriendly or that we are disadvantaged victims of circumstances. But do we want to think differently? Here, we might begin to ask ourselves some probing questions. *Is it helping me to think this way? Might things be better if I developed different beliefs about the world and about others? What would it take for me to believe that, for example, I need not be a victim?*

It is here that inspirational ideas help calm our worries. Many a morning and night, I saw my parents on their knees asking God for guidance and help in difficult times. An inspirational book, talk, or sermon challenges negative beliefs and helps us to see that there is another way to think. When that happens, we find our hearts are warmed with hope because we are no longer trapped in our old patterns of feeling and thought.

My friend Anthony was feeling panicked about money and wondered how he could ever pay his bills and make ends meet. Staying at a friend's house, he turned on the television and happened on a program where an evangelical minister was talking about prosperity. The minister's theme was that we can pray all we want for material abundance, but if we are inconsiderate of others in the small details of our lives we block our prosperity. Anthony realized that he had not been as considerate of his friends and family as he should. He realized that he had been taking them for granted and that with very little effort he could be kinder and more loving to them. Both his mind and his heart were touched and he began to make some changes. As he did so, he saw all of his circumstances in a new light and saw that there were resources at his disposal—including financial resources—that he had not seen before.

I have taken a great deal of time discussing worry for a couple of reasons. First, worry is something many of us do a great deal, without realizing that we can turn it to our advantage. And second, worry is not that much different from many other things in the heart's garden: we think of them as weeds, but they are really flowers.

∞

When the mind steps in to till the garden in your heart, you can use the full range of the heart's feelings while creating positive and helpful beliefs about yourself and the world. These can get us through the tough times. The power of an idea to propel us through difficulties is amazing. The step across the threshold from raw feeling to positive belief is a most significant one. Yet it is not the fullest level of life experience.

There is yet another threshold to cross—from the mind to the soul. Like Virgil taking Dante to the edge of Paradise, the mind can help us and console us and bring us truth in times of confusion—but by itself it cannot lead us into the territory of the soul. The mind is close to the soul—the center of eternal truth and value—because the mind deals with universals and how they apply to individual situations. The mind deals in syllogisms, telling us how to go from universal truths to particular instances, or how to discover universal rules from particular moments. When we actually cross the threshold into living soulfully, however, we learn how to live and experience the wholeness of things. We experience an inner joy and peace in which the feelings of the heart and the truth of the mind come together.

Let's take an example. When I was hurt and betrayed by some colleagues years ago (you can find the details in *Good News for Bad Days*), my raw and wounded heart was ready for revenge. My mind took stock of my heart's desires and showed me that the best thing to do was to leave revenge to God and instead to focus on what was best for my life. Now that was fine and good, and it got me to make some good decisions about going to the next parish, getting involved in radio and community work, and so on, even though my heart was still raw at times.

But there was a level of insight and of living that I was yet to attain. Only years later did I come to understand that somehow that experience was meant to move me in a new direction—to being a radio host, a writer and speaker, and a much wiser and better priest and human being. It took me even longer to realize that my coming out of tragedy into this new direction was not just a matter of blind exception, but was an invitation to see that my entire life was a call and an opportunity to experience beauty and the joy of service. It was as though I had been taken to life's inner sanctum to discover its inner working and secrets.

I've been speaking of the garden in the heart, and true gardeners will understand what I mean by this inner sanctum, for there are various levels to gardening. At one level, gardens are groupings of various kinds of flowers, which we see and say, "Oh, that's beautiful" and pass on. At another level, gardening is a science, and you can spend hours reading gardening books and tuning in to garden programs on radio and television. From these, you learn the rules that will help you to best care for your garden. But one day, you walk into your garden and suddenly are struck by the miracle of how dirt and seeds and toil and sweat have produced roses and tulips and daffodils and petunias and snapdragons and geraniums. We're not really gardeners until we have been touched by the miracle of it all.

But the truth is, we have been gardeners all along, and the miracle has been there all along—we just haven't seen it until now.

That's how it is with the rest of life, too. The miracle—what author Wayne Dyer calls "real magic"—is there when we are defeated, discouraged, downhearted, sick, and exhausted. It is there when we sit down with our therapist or our clergyperson or our stacks of journals and books in an effort to sort out our feelings and find clarity. But just as there is a point where gardeners become *real* gardeners in the soul as well as in the soil, so there is a point in life where we stop "hanging in there" and "coping" and surrender to the true magic of life. The magic consists in our taking the garden of our heart and being awestruck by its charm, its variety, its challenges, its seasons, and its ability to at times exhaust and stump us. We are taken with the wonder of it all.

The gardens of my boyhood and the gardens of my maturity have taught me how to heartstorm. My heart is a garden. I am a gardener. There are magic and mystery and invisible hands that guide me as I plant my feet in the soil of life every single day.

CHAPTER THREE

Cordiality

Recalling Phil from Howard Beach

I cannot think of cordiality—one of the principal qualities of the heart—without thinking of my friend Phil Salberg, or "Phil from Howard Beach," as he was known to his radio friends. I can't remember the first time Phil called me on the radio, but I know that we knew each other for over five years in all. His warm and friendly personality, his quick wit, and his vibrant concern for others profoundly touched my heart. It turned out that my radio programs "As You Think" and "Religion on the Line" were by no means the only programs Phil called. In fact, Phil was on almost every radio station in the city. An avid sports fan, he was a regular on many of the shows on WFAN, an all-sports station in New York City. His ability to talk in depth about sports was truly amazing. His weekday mornings were spent listening to Bill Mazer on WEVD, and he frequently called to lock horns with "The Amazin'" Mazer. I seem to recall his talking to someone on WLIB, an urban talk station in Manhattan.

Somewhere along the way, Phil got connected with WGBB on Long Island and became friendly with Joey Alcarese, an overnight talk host who later became station manager. Joey is a devout Christian woman who is deeply impassioned about the issue of the abuse of women. One of her shows was dedicated to discussing abuse. Her gentle manner appealed to Phil, and before long he was a regular listener and regular caller. When I was a guest on the program, Phil, on the phone, was like a co-host, asking questions and joining in the trialogue. Joey was one of the many with whom Phil bridged the gap between Christians and Jews.

Over the years, Phil from Howard Beach became an important part of my radio life. Every Saturday night, I could count on a phone call from him on "As You Think." Regardless of the topic, Phil always had a timely and interesting comment or question. Phil engaged each guest, whether famous or little known, with intelligence and respect. Every Sunday morning that I hosted "Religion on the Line" on WABC, I would look at my computer screen and there would be Phil, waiting for his turn on the air.

Phil's range of knowledge was astounding. It seemed he could talk to anybody about anything. What was even more amazing was his phenomenal ability to respect others even when he profoundly disagreed with them. One time, a caller on another station said some fairly mean things about Phil on the air; Phil got his phone number and called him, and the two became fast friends. That was his way. It was his earnest desire to make friends with everyone.

It was not long before Phil from Howard Beach became much more than a listener and caller; he became a dear friend. He would call me at work on Tuesdays and Fridays at about 3:30 in the afternoon, just to check in and see how I was. If he couldn't get me, he would try and try again until he succeeded. He literally wanted to hear my voice and to know that I was all right. He had two questions for me. One, who was going to be on "As You Think" the following Saturday? Two, who was going to be host of "Religion on the Line" on Sunday? "Who's got the button this week?" he would ask before one of our Roundtable Sundays. He would get annoyed if I had a taped program scheduled, because that would deprive him of a chance to call in.

Through these conversations, I learned so much about this wonderful man who came to touch my heart so deeply. I learned that he was blind, had been blind for many years, and that the telephone and the radio were his lifelines. I was always amazed that he was so cheerful and upbeat, that he accepted his disability with such peace of soul. He never complained or inclined you to feel sorry for him. On the contrary, he always tried to make you feel better, and at times even joked about his blindness. Once there was a chance that a particular course of treatment might restore his sight, and he went to the ophthalmologist full of hope. It was not to be. Yet not for one minute did he cry or complain. He accepted his blindness as naturally as he accepted breathing.

Phil and I often talked about our cats. He adored his cats, pretty much as I loved mine. They would hop up on the bed and he would stroke them and feel their fur, all the while listening to their purring. Feeding the cats and changing the litter were among his tasks in the household, and he treated them as a privilege rather than as chores. One day he called me in tears to tell me that his beloved cat Merry had died.

Phil loved his family, and they in turn have become dear friends of mine. Marsha, his wife of forty years, is a solid bedrock whose hearty nature, unfailing sense of humor, and scrumptious matzo ball soup bring life and cheer to any situation. His son Martin—now a dear friend in his own right—was that wonderful son who was always dropping by the house to see what he could do for Mom and Dad. It is Martin now who calls me at work on Tuesdays and Fridays as "Martin from Howard Beach" on the radio. Tori, Martin's lovely wife, was as beloved to Phil as if she had been his own daughter. Phil and I often talked about children, and he was impassioned about sensitive parenting and treating children right. A lot of that came from his infant son, Ian, whose tragic death touched Phil deeply.

Though we talked several times a week, I met Phil only twice—once at my fiftieth birthday party and once in the hospital. He was so happy to be at my party, and he proudly gave me a black T-shirt with the inscription "World's Greatest Father," which I keep to this day.

Phil's friends were legion, and he was fiercely loyal to them all. A little coterie of friends developed around fellow talk radio callers, and eventually some of them became my friends as well. If a host on a radio station treated one of those friends unkindly, he would receive an angry call from Phil, telling him in no uncertain terms that he was not to do that again. A group of those friends were invited—not once, but twice—to the WGBB studios to conduct a roundtable, and some of them were the subjects of a documentary that aired on public access television in the New York area. I have a picture of Phil sitting behind the mike at WGBB, looking happy and perfectly in his element.

One person Phil truly admired was John Cardinal O'Connor, then Archbishop of New York. He often spoke in glowing terms about the Cardinal and how he had embraced people of the Jewish faith. When Cardinal O'Connor became ill, not a phone conversation went by without Phil's asking me how the Cardinal was that day. On days when I had a bad report to give him, his distress was obvious.

In 1998 and 1999, Phil developed some fairly serious health problems. He always battled back, and I would hear from him before, after, and sometimes during his hospital stays. If he couldn't call me himself, Martin would call to update me on his father's condition. He seemed to be doing well until April 2000, when he began to experience painful swelling in his leg, so much so that he found it nearly impossible to walk. When he called me, he would often be seized with a racking cough that prevented him from speaking. I was getting worried about my friend.

On April 15, I was interviewing Thomas Moore, whose beautiful books on soulful living are well known on "As You Think." I had been later than usual getting to the station, and when Phil called to talk before the show, I had to ask Holly, my screener, to say I'd talk to him later. Holly had come to know Phil from the show, and confided to me that he sounded terrible. When I went to Phil's call during the show, I was at least somewhat prepared for the high-pitched, hoarse voice that came from my friend. He asked what Thomas Moore called a terrific question, about the soulfulness of suffering; and I knew that question had come directly from Phil's heart. Phil called me, as usual, after the show; and it was obvious that he was in terrible agony. He assured me that he was seeing the doctor the following week. I thanked him for calling me when he was in such pain. His response was, "Father Paul, the Saturday night or Sunday morning you don't hear from me, you'll know I'm no longer here." I shuddered, and told him I wanted to talk to him early in the week.

Phil called me on Monday, sounding a little better, and promising me that he was going to the doctor on Tuesday. Again I thanked him for calling while in pain, and again he told me, "If you don't hear from me, it's because I'm no longer here." That was to be our last conversation. When Phil went to the doctor on Tuesday, he was admitted to the cardiac intensive care unit of the hospital with congestive heart failure and kidney problems. Martin called me with daily reports. On Saturday night, Phil told Marsha and Martin to be sure to listen to "As You Think" on the way home from the hospital. When we had spoken on Monday, I had told him I was rebroadcasting an interview with my high school teachers, Sisters Raymond and Rita, in which Phil and Marsha had played a prominent part. He wanted to be sure they heard it.

Sunday, Phil began to experience severe anxiety attacks, and it became necessary to medicate him. When I visited him in the hospital on Wednesday night, he was on a respirator and was sound asleep. I chatted with Marsha, and when it was time to leave, I gave my Jewish friend a Catholic blessing and touched his cheek for the last time. On Saturday, Martin called me on "As You Think" to tell my listeners and me that his father had died.

Phil's funeral was just what he had told me he wanted. A couple of years before, he had talked to my good friend Rabbi Joseph Potasnik and me about the arrangements. "Father Paul, I don't want any long-winded clergymen speaking about me," he announced. And so, in the Lockwood Funeral Home in Brooklyn, a packed roomful of family and friends gathered around his plain pine box and, led by Martin and by Phil's brother Melvin, celebrated Phil's life and prayed him home.

The day after Phil's funeral, on May 3, 2000, Cardinal O'Connor died. I smile when I think of Phil from Howard Beach welcoming His Eminence past the pearly gates.

∞

The word *cordial* comes from the Latin word *cor*, meaning "heart." The dictionary tells us that cordiality is "the quality of being warmly and genially affable." When I wanted to heartstorm about cordiality, Phil was the first person who came to mind. Talking to Phil, people were impressed by the breadth of his knowledge, but most especially they were impressed by the largesse of his heart. He could talk fondly to anyone, even to those with whom he disagreed.

That is the essence of cordiality, and when the mind looks to know the virtues of the heart, it is cordiality that it looks for most of all. One of the most striking things about the heart is that it holds within itself such a wide range of feelings. It is amazing how quickly we can go from one feeling to another. One minute the heart is full of happiness, and the next second it is raging against some slight or injustice. The heart plays host to a wide variety of feelings and impressions. It must allow each of them time and space to be itself, in the same way that a good host makes room for his guests. The heart simultaneously hosts a variety of guests, many of whom may be in conflict with one another. Cordiality is that quality of the heart that enables all of those feelings to coexist without destroying one another or the heart itself.

Thinking of Phil from Howard Beach puts me in mind of the wide range of the heart's contents. As I mentioned, Phil called in to a broad spectrum of programs—shows that covered sports, politics, and spirituality and religion. He not only knew a great deal about each subject, but he had passion for each. When we're in touch with our hearts, we find there a wide range of passions about a number of things.

Phil enjoyed his passions, and it's important for us to enjoy ours. Sometimes a wide range of strong feelings about many things can confuse or frighten us. When the mind learns that this is normal, the heart can relax and enjoy its diversity.

Some conflicts will need to be resolved, and the mind can help the heart to do this. The key question the mind can give the heart is, *What do I really want for myself and for everyone else in this situation?* For example, a man may be reasonably happy in his marriage, and then meet a woman who sends him head over heels in love. Now he feels conflicted and guilty. He loves his wife and feels guilty about his feelings for the other woman. He may, at the same time, find himself angry with his wife for ways in which she appears not to measure up to his new love.

In order to handle this situation properly, the man must do two things. First, he must acknowledge all of the feelings involved. If he denies any of the feelings, he's in trouble. He must acknowledge the ways in which he loves his wife, the things about her that annoy him and the positive feelings he has for the other woman.

Second, he must refrain from taking hasty action. If he runs from his feelings for the other woman and goes back to his marriage without fully understanding what he is doing, he is likely to be tempted to leave his marriage over and over again. If, morals not withstanding, he decides to run from the marriage into the arms of his new love, he may find himself with deeply unresolved issues that will make it hard for him to fully commit to the new love.

Instead, he must acknowledge the conflict and sort out what is behind it. What is best for him and for everyone in this situation?

The mind will contribute a number of things to clarify the storms of the heart. One of these is the notion of the importance of honoring commitments. At the moment, the man in our story does not feel like honoring his marriage, but his mind tells him—re-*minds* him—that feeling or not feeling like it is not the final consideration. He made a sacred commitment to his wife until death do them part. That commitment is not terminated simply because he has met someone else. With that information, his mind can bring some clarity to the conflicted feelings of his heart. He knows now that he must work on reviving his marriage.

How he does that will be greatly influenced by what he knows about relationships. If he thinks, for instance, that he can improve his marriage by changing his wife's behavior (say, by criticizing or correcting her), that is what he will do. More than likely, however, his heart will respond with resentment and frustration as his wife resists taking the blame for their problems and perhaps retaliates by criticizing him in return.

With better information, he learns that the best way to improve his marriage is to change himself. There is much less frustration and greater satisfaction in this, for two reasons: one, the only person he can really change is himself; two, as he grows within himself, his wife will likely notice the changes and respond accordingly. Susan Zappo brought this amazing fact to my attention through her pioneering work in Marriage Restoration. In this unique approach, Susan often works with only one partner in a troubled marriage. She has seen miracles when one spouse learns how to improve his or her own attitude and how to develop new skills in communication and in the art of expressing love. The other spouse notices, and things change.

Having the right information about what it takes to change himself and to save his marriage, the husband in our story will find his heart taking a correction course. That doesn't mean that he will not still have feelings for the other woman, or that he won't get frustrated with his wife sometimes. It does mean that his mind will help his heart to grow in cordiality—in developing a sincere and natural ease of manner—because it is giving the turbulence of his heart's feelings a different focus and direction from before. He has *confidence*—literally "faith with" himself—and that confi-

dence radiates to all around him. I use Phil from Howard
Beach as an image of that cordial confidence because he
reflected that ease with himself and so could draw others to
him and turn enemies into friends. The cordial mind, in a
similar fashion, welcomes conflicting feelings into its horizons and brings them to resolution.

∞

When the mind and heart are working in tandem, there arises
the possibility of crossing the threshold of the soul. The
soul—the unifying spiritual life principle—has, of course,
been there all along, but it has gone more or less unnoticed.
As the man in our example and his wife develop a more loving union with each other, they begin to notice that their
marriage takes on a new life of its own. Before, their marriage had been kind of a day in, day out living arrangement;
now there is a magic about it. They may disagree and argue
from time to time, but even these setbacks remind them that
they are a team and that they are really on the same side.
They also know better and more naturally how to respond to
the other's moods, needs, and gifts. They find themselves
learning to compromise and are surprised to learn that doing
so does not mean that they lose or lose out.

This transformation of their marriage into a union of
their minds and hearts can best be described as crossing into
its soul. I often advise married couples to treat their marriage
like an entity unto itself. For it is: a marriage is a union of

souls that elicits the best and noblest in each soul by drawing both souls together. The soul of a marriage does not compromise the souls of the spouses, but gently transforms them.

This is soulful cordiality. Once the magic of the soul has been discovered, we embrace the mind and the heart in a new way. Where once the heart was chaotic and confounded, where once the mind was rigid, now they easily and effortlessly feed the soul and inspire us to look for guidance in the smallest details of our lives. Living in the soul, our hearts and minds—our entire lives—take on a depth and dimension unknown to us before. Like Phil from Howard Beach, we are able to embrace both the good and the bad and welcome both into the substance of our lives.

We become truly cordial.

CHAPTER FOUR

The Tortured Heart

The Heartstorming of Job

"Man," wrote Erich Fromm, "is the only animal for whom his own existence is a problem which he has to solve." Much of life has to do with solving problems. Fromm was talking about a specific set of problems—those that bring into question our very existence. We worry about things because they appear to us to threaten our existence.

That is what happens when fear overtakes us. We feel as if we are being strangled by our problems and are unable to breathe. We become afraid for our marriage, or fret about money, or fear for our children, jobs, health, or safety. Before we know it, we are, as we say, all tied up in knots.

I am admittedly no stranger to fear. Through college, seminary, and graduate school, I was constantly afraid I would fail. In my first years in radio, I had fears about not having enough money to air "As You Think" and having it go off the air as a result.

Fear can be a good thing. It can motivate us to look out for our well-being. If we weren't afraid to some extent about our health, we would scarcely bother to take care of ourselves. Fear over money can lead us to spend wisely and invest shrewdly. Fear for the safety of our children can prevent us from taking excessive risks with their health and well-being. Fear for our jobs can help us to do them more diligently.

How or why do we cross the line to the point where fear overcomes us? It's as Fromm described it: we fear excessively when somehow our existence feels threatened.

Advertisers know this. On the surface, the ads we see and hear may tell us about a product or a service, but at much deeper levels they often make us feel threatened, that without the product we will not be able to handle life or win the approving glances of our peers.

It is an unfortunate fact of life that there are people who essentially want to bully us, to scare us into thinking that they are more powerful than we and can wipe us out. Even more unfortunately, many of us are conditioned to feel that life and its challenges are larger than we are and that life is an ongoing battle in which we are pitted against forces bigger than we are. We become accustomed to thinking that life is just that way. "As you think, so shall you be," the Bible tells us. As our hearts become accustomed to cowering, we often read threats into situations where nothing was intended. We believe that life is out to get us.

Sometimes it really does seem as if life is out to get us. The story of Job in the Bible is a perfect example of what happens when our worst fears are realized, and how our hearts and those of others respond in the face of that. When Job loses everything and his loved ones die, he is bewildered because he knows that he did nothing to deserve such a fate. His wife wants no part of his attitude of innocence and counsels him, "Curse God and die!" Job answers her wisely, saying, "Shall we accept good from God, and not trouble?"

Nonetheless, Job is devastated, deeply broken in spirit, so much so that when his friends come to console him, they barely recognize him. In fact, they do something wonderful—they sit with him in silence for seven days and seven nights. You and I might be tempted to offer advice—those wise friends sit in silent accompaniment.

After seven days, Job's desolation erupts. He curses the day on which he was born. In a telling remark, Job says, "What I feared has come upon me." Indeed, our worries can create the very thing that we dread. We are left to wonder whether perhaps Job had worried over the years about losing his family and possessions.

Job's lament is too much for Eliphaz the Temanite, who can keep silent no longer. He tells Job to be reasonable: no one who is truly innocent has endured such devastation as Job experienced. How can Job claim to be an innocent victim? Instead of blaming God, Job should turn to God, who "wounds but he also binds up; he injures, but his hands also heal."

Job's response is that of a victim. "Do I have any power," he laments, "to help myself, now that success has been driven from me?" Reading between the lines, we again get an insight into Job's attitude of heart. It is clear that his ideas of success meant having a large family and lots of possessions. Now that they are gone, he feels like a failure. "I despise my life," he wails. "I would not live forever . . . my days have no meaning." He demands that God leave him alone, but ironically he also says that he will not stop crying out. That's how we feel when we are brokenhearted: we want to be left alone, but we need to cry out, to talk to somebody.

Job's second friend, Bildad the Shuhite, advises Job to stop complaining and to turn to God, to plead with him. But Job feels helpless before God: "God does not restrain his anger. . . . How then can I dispute with him?" Job feels utterly helpless, yet he vows to cry out his victimhood to God. When his third friend, Zophar the Naamathite, challenges him, "Can you fathom the mysteries of God?" Job replies with yet another expression of victimhood: "I have become a laughing stock to my friends. . . ." Besides, Job argues, what can he do when God has destroyed everything? "What he tears

down," Job cries, "cannot be built up." Yet again, Job vows
to take his case to God. Eliphaz tells him not to be so foolish, but Job remonstrates, "If I speak, my pain is not heard,
and if I refrain it does not go away." Still, his friends try to
dissuade him from railing against God. Nonetheless, Job,
deeply wounded, persists in maintaining his innocence until,
at last, "the three men stopped answering Job, because he was
righteous in his own eyes."

Elihu, whose presence is not mentioned until this point
in the story, steps forward to condemn Job for rebelling
against God, specifically the rebellion of claiming to know
God's incomprehensible ways. At last, poor Job is questioned
by God himself. In the end, the mystery of God's oversee-
ing of all things calms Job, and he realizes he has spoken of
things beyond his understanding. He apologizes to God. God
restores his fortunes.

At the level of the heart, what has happened to Job?
Clearly he has been devastated and has lost his bearings. At
first, he is reduced to silence: he sits in sackcloth and ashes,
unable to speak. When he finally does speak, his words are
tortured and racked with pain. Like those of us who have lost
our bearings in life at one time or other, Job's words reflect
the contradictory feelings that are in his heart. Sometimes he
says that he is going to give God a piece of his mind . . . at
other times he feels like a victim: God is powerful, so how
could Job dare to speak to him, especially to complain? Just

about the only consistency in Job's feelings is his profound insistence upon his innocence. That indeed is the core of his problem: he believes—indeed knows—that he is innocent, and for that reason he simply cannot understand why such terrible things have befallen him.

Job's heart is a heart in pain and turmoil. Just as Luther said about the human heart in general, Job's heart "is like a ship on a stormy sea driven about by winds blowing from all four corners of heaven."

Job's friends, Eliphaz, Bildad, and Zophar, represent three attempts of the mind to deal with the heart's pain. At first they say nothing to him. Often in the face of searing pain the mind is numb, dumbfounded at the chaos and the crisis. When the friends do speak, they attempt to bring Job to his senses. In three cycles of speeches each tries to tell Job that he would not have experienced such devastating losses if he were innocent. Indeed, he *must* have done something to incur the wrath of God. The logic of the mind says that instead of protesting that he is innocent, Job should acknowledge his wrongdoing and confess it before God. He should see the devastation as an invitation to repent.

What is happening here is that the mind is trying to help the heart to make sense of what has happened. Any of us who have experienced losses know that this is what we do. After an initial period of being stunned, we try to make sense of our feelings by trying to find a logical explanation for them. Years ago, when I was betrayed by those colleagues in ministry, I initially tried to make sense of the situation by proposing that maybe they were right. Maybe I deserved to be treated that way; maybe I even deserved their harsh judgment. Maybe everybody who over the years had said I was hopeless were right after all. People do the same thing after the loss of a loved one. How often have I heard family members blame themselves—if only they had done more, if only they had been there, if only they had prayed harder, perhaps their loved one would still be alive. Job's friends are right in the same line, and it's a natural and perfectly understandable way of trying to make sense of what the heart feels to be senseless.

There is another speaker, as we saw earlier, who appears out of nowhere. Interestingly, his function in the story is to anticipate the speech of God. He tells Job and his friends that God's ways are mysterious and unfathomable to human beings. Moreover, he says, God is sublime and great beyond all knowledge. It is for us to revere him and his ways, not to challenge them.

Reading the Book of Job, I see in Elihu's speech the effort of human intelligence to bring us to the verge of soulfulness without actually crossing over into it. Later, Dante did something similar in *The Divine Comedy*, allowing Virgil to bring him to the edge of Paradise, but not into Paradise. The human mind can organize and calm the heart, but all the ideas and reasoning in the world cannot bring us across the threshold of the soul, into the mystery of life itself. When we encounter misfortune, we typically try to find the reasons that it happened—but is it really possible to know? The mind can only take us so far. Elihu adds an important dimension to what human reasoning can offer in the face of Job's crisis. Nonetheless, his opinion is still the opinion of a human being. It is not the opinion of God.

∞

It isn't until chapter 38 that God enters the discussion of Job's tragedy. Of course, he is there all along, but in silence. That is what we have been saying about the soul, the locus of the divine and eternal in life. It is there all along, but there comes a point where we become aware of its presence and importance in our lives. I was well into my forties before I began to reflect seriously on the nature of the soul, but my soul was there all along, waiting for me to discover its guidance and to pay attention to it.

It is important to notice how the author of the Book of Job describes God's entry into the fray. Chapter 38 begins: "Then the LORD answered Job out of the storm." From everything that has happened, we might expect God to be depicted as above and beyond the fray. Instead, he speaks right from the midst of it. The dynamic of the Book of Job is reminiscent of Robert Frost's poem "The Secret Sits": "We all sit around in a ring and suppose / But the secret sits in the middle, and knows."

God's speaking from the midst of the storm is important, because that fact corrects the image of God, who throughout the story has been portrayed as being far above and beyond the ways of man, practically unchallengeable. God has been around all through Job's crisis, not merely at the end of the story. Just as I've been saying that the soul is always there even though we don't always consult it, so the author of Job is saying the same thing about God. God was there in chapters 3 to 37, even though Job and his friends—the human heart and mind—did not see him.

Notice, too, how God deals with Job. Job's friends have been giving him answers. Instead, God tells Job, "I will question you, and you tell me the answers." Here we thought God had all the answers. Instead, God has all the questions! The direction of the questions is most interesting, creating awe and wonder at the mystery of creation and how creation came to be as it did. That's exactly what a soulful approach to loss or grievance or injustice does—it takes the hard core of hurt feelings and definite answers that we receive from the heart and the mind and softens them by setting these terrible events as part of the overall wonder of creation.

How does this work? When I was so terribly hurt by those colleagues of mine, my heart was a mess and my mind raged against the injustice of it all. I later came to see that this whole bizarre episode was one phase of a total reconstruction of my life, in which my health improved, my skills in writing and in radio emerged, and I entered into a new phase of ministry. This is exactly what God did with Job—he put his sorrow into the context of the wonder of creation and re-created Job's life.

God did this by asking questions, not by giving answers; and that is what the soul often does as well. The soul won't necessarily tell us, "Take that job" or "Consult that person." It might point us to some poetry or to a piece of music, or lead us to overhear a chance remark. *Are these coincidences?* we ask. That's precisely what God did with Job—he pointed him to a host of natural occurrences and in essence asked him, "Are these merely coincidences?" He led Job into wonder, into the life of the soul. And he allowed Job to put his pain there as part of the overall mystery of creation.

That is not all. If we know anything about the great religious stories of life, we know that once you have faced God, you must retrace your steps and return to the point from which you came. The encounter with God transforms the mind: God punishes the three who gave Job false and misleading ideas. It also transforms the heart. Job says, "therefore I despise myself and repent in dust and ashes." The phrase *despise myself* in the translation (New International Version) may seem a bit harsh to our ears. Other translations go the route of having Job say that he repudiates what he said. But the New International Version translation is useful, for the self that Job repudiates is his old self. Now he is a new self, transformed by his entry into the realm of soul. It's nice to be able to say, "I don't care for the person I was years ago. I'm glad I've deepened and matured."

The Book of Job is, in essence, a portrayal of the nature of heartstorming—the journey from heart to mind to soul and back again. It is one man's story, but every man's and every woman's as well. It tells us that no matter how fettered we may become as a result of our fears when they come true, our hearts can become unshackled by the power of the mind and the subtlety of the soul.

CHAPTER FIVE

Sentimental
Helping the Mind to Feel

My father was the first person to teach me the true meaning of sentimentality. It may be my imagination, but the early 1960s—the period after Vatican II made enormous changes in the life of the Catholic Church—seemed to be the start of my father's career as a curmudgeon. He bought very little of Vatican II, and even less of the young priests of our parish. One in particular drew Dad's wrath— a really bright young man who gave the impression of being intellectually superior to everyone. One day this young iconoclast was pontificating about sentimentality and describing it from the pulpit as something weak, a quality that truly strong, mature people don't give in to. I could see the blood rising in my father's face; and when we got home, his Irish temper came on full blast. "What does that young whipper-snapper *mean* by talking like that?" he bellowed. "Why, sentimentality is not something weak, it's something strong!"

I wasn't sure I agreed with Dad at the time, but as I matured I realized that he was right, as he so often was. When I watched Mom support him in his crises, when I watched him nurse her through cancer to a painful death, I knew that sentimentality was a virtue, not a weakness. It's an insight that has served me well in the years since.

Now, there is, of course, a kind of schmaltz that can arise from extreme sentimentality, where one gets overly emotional about someone or something. Unfortunately, this often becomes confused with genuine sentimentality and mistaken for it. "Sentimentalists," wrote Emerson, "adopt whatever merit is in good repute and almost make it hateful with their praise."

There is a difference between sentimentalism, as Emerson described it, and genuine sentimentality. Most of us, including the young preacher on that fateful day, tend to ignore that difference. Genuine sentiment is the key to the heart. When the heart is sentimental, it is doing what a heart should be doing—treasuring someone or something, honoring it, and feeding that honor to the mind and ultimately to the soul.

The word *sentimental* literally means "feeling mind" or "a mind that feels." To be sentimental in the fullest sense of the word means to know something with feeling, with passion.

The difference between sentimentality and sentimentalism lies in the right balance between the feelings and the mind. Sentimentalism uses the concepts of the mind to fuel the fires of the heart. True sentimentality does not need to fan any flames; both words and silence flow from the warm admiration the heart feels. We see the difference immediately at a funeral. How many times have we listened to a eulogy and wondered whether the speaker ever met the person he was eulogizing? French mime Marcel Marceau, who spent his life communicating through silence, had it right when he said, "Do not the most moving moments of our lives find us all without words?" After the death of John Cardinal O'Connor, I heard many eloquent and fitting tributes to this remarkable man. To me, the most eloquent of them all came from Eileen White, the Cardinal's longtime counsel. I happened to meet Eileen in the Catholic Center offices the day after the Cardinal's death. With tears in her eyes, she embraced me and said, "We have lost our friend." That was the tribute to Cardinal O'Connor that I most needed to hear. That is true sentiment—when the feelings and the words reflect each other.

Why did the word *sentimental* come to have such a weak connotation? It's hard to pinpoint it precisely, but to some extent it may be traced to a kind of hardening of our society in the twentieth century. For all the advances made in science, technology, and communications, the world became, emotionally speaking, a tougher place in which to live and work. In an information-rich society, knowledge and achievement are fervently emphasized. As the frontiers of knowledge expand, it is the mind and not the heart that often takes precedence. We hear people talk about following their hearts, but we know full well that they had better have plenty of smarts, plenty of information, and plenty of chutzpah if they're going to succeed.

Let's face it—there's a lot of toughness in our world, and all too often it seems to divide people rather than bring them together. I am appalled by the amount of racial and religious bias that exists today, often spoken loudly and unapologetically. We have made great progress in race relations as a society, and diverse peoples are relating to one another better than ever before—but the amount of prejudice that still exists is staggering.

A phenomenon that has done more than almost anything else to break down the barriers to fellow feeling is storytelling. When people on opposite sides can sit down and hear each other's stories, a mutual sentiment arises that cuts across religious, ethnic, and cultural barriers. One reason for this is that the familiarity in the stories we tell transcends differences. In her remarkable book *Jump Time*, Jean Houston tells of a woman named Leah Green who has facilitated peace among Jews and Muslims in the Middle East by arranging for them to hear each other's stories—for example, childhood stories about grandparents. Before long, people who began as enemies come to realize that they have much in common and begin to see that their differences need not block understanding.

I have seen something similar in my own experiences of people from different faith groups. As a small child, I lived in a neighborhood where a large number of Jews moved and settled. Before long, synagogues, Jewish schools, and a Jewish home for the aged dotted the neighborhood, and you could hear Yiddish in the streets. This was nearly fifty years ago; and sadly, many Gentiles moved away, not wanting to live in what they had come to consider "a Jewish neighborhood." What a missed opportunity!

I thought of this recently while sitting around the dining room table of my dear friends Lisa and Wayne Dicksteen. It was Passover, and they and their son, Jordan, had invited me to take part in the Seder celebration of freedom with their family and friends. As we told the Passover story—Lisa invited everyone around the table to participate—and shared in the ritual, I realized that I was hearing the stories of Jews yesterday, but also the stories of the people with whom I was sitting—young people, old people, struggling to keep their traditions alive against the secularism that tempts us away from them. During the meal, someone said to me, "Father, this is the story of everyone, not only of Jews," and he was right.

On another level, I realized that the Passover story is one of the triumph of freedom over anything that kills the human spirit; and that we Jews and Christians around the table were telling stories that pointed to the overriding struggle for freedom that is ours. As I write, there is a terrible struggle being waged against slavery in the Sudan, one the media has largely deemed unmarketable. Over the years I have come to know many people who suffer the ravages of mental illness, and who often cannot tell what is objectively real from the wild roller coasters that power their minds. There, too, is the universal human story of struggle for freedom. It, too, is recounted in the Jewish Seder and in the Catholic celebration of the Mass.

In this age of heartstorming, this twenty-first century of ours, we need to discover that sentimentality is a positive. More and more we need those feeling minds that take us away from hatred and prejudice and allow us to feel the beat of the universal heart. Not long ago, I saw in a magazine a story about a young woman who, though deaf, is a percussionist. She performs barefoot so that she can feel the rhythms of the music in her feet and keep time. Sentimental people—people with hearts and minds that feel the universal rhythms and concrete circumstances of their lives—are true icons of this age of heartstorming. They are the ones whose compassion enables them to cross the barriers of hatred and prejudice and to hear the drumbeat of freedom amidst the cacophony of oppression. It is only sensible to do so.

Sensible is another word that evokes the feeling, sentimental mind. We think that something is sensible when its use is reasonable or rational. We wear sensible shoes if we are sensible people.

In truth, *sensible* means to be connected to the feelings. Something is sensible, in the primary sense of the word, if it can be felt. If we bring the two meanings together, it is sensible to be able to feel and to enjoy the passion and information that the feelings bring to life. Heartstormers are sensible people who approach the world with sentiment, with compassionate hearts.

∞

What is the nature of the mind that feels and that is truly sentimental?

As we become comfortable with living in the twenty-first century, we find ourselves entering into more worlds than we dared to dream of before. When I started "As You Think" in 1992, I was not alone in not owning a personal computer or having access to the Internet. It was two years later that my friend Professor Polly Guerin called me and said, "Father, you simply *must* go down and buy yourself a ThinkPad." At about the same time, I was asked by an Internet service provider to host a chat room for them. I was being led into cyberspace. My primitive laptop had a 2400 modem and a monochrome screen, but it got me going. Access to the Internet opened a whole world of important information. My little laptop was slow but very effective: it amazed me that one little box could open to so much.

I quickly learned that hosting chat rooms and hosting talk radio shows were very different. Talk radio is generally a one-on-one—one host to one caller at a time. As a host, you finish with one caller and to go the next, and so on. In a chat room, all the "callers" are there at once. You can have multiple conversations going on simultaneously. When I was a kid, I remember my teacher saying, "You can't do two things at once!" In a chat room, both hosts and participants have to be able to pay attention to many things going on at the same time. This means that the "feeling mind" must stay attuned to a chef's salad of conversations, all the while being able to distinguish the carrots from the lettuce from the celery from the tomatoes.

What complicates things even further is that some of the conversations in a chat room tend to be negative and destructive in nature. The participant is anonymous in cyberspace, and entry onto the information superhighway often unleashes the cyberequivalent of road rage. It's not just that the mind has to be mental—it has to be *senti*-mental to feel out which conversations are helpful, which are salacious, and which are downright harmful. As a kid I remember thanking God for designing our ears so that we didn't have to hear all the conversation simultaneously going on in the world. In a chat room, you are exposed to the entire global village and all of its conversations at once, then asked to feel out its various elements, to think about them, and to keep a thread going— all at the same time. Once I did a chat room with a minister and a rabbi, both of whom remarked how exhausted they were at the end of the hour. It is a workout!

The feeling mind—the mind that knows in connection with the heart—is like a chat room host. It must learn to turn its multifacetedness to its advantage. This is where the mind and the heart truly meld, for the mind revels in the heart's diversity and multiplicity. To keep both heart and mind from running out of gas, the soul must join them and do what they cannot.

Indeed, if human beings are going to thrive rather than succumb to the potentially overwhelming plethora of challenges to our minds and hearts, this mind-heart melding of authentic sentimentality is a must. Jean Houston argues in *Jump Time* that we must learn to turn our diversity from a draining disadvantage into a powerful advantage. She calls this becoming *polyphrenic*, as opposed to schizophrenic. The root *phrenia* refers to the mind. Instead of becoming overwhelmed by the multiplex nature of our lives, Dr. Houston suggests, we should draw upon and even unite our various energies so that instead of being segregated and compartmentalized, they become united. For example, I am a parish priest, a writer, a radio host, a fund-raiser, a cat parent, a spiritual adviser, a radio aficionado, a cook, and so on. If I keep these identities separated in their own compartments, I am likely to become overwhelmed and exhausted in both heart and mind. There is just too much to do. I am also likely to become blocked in one or more of these areas from time to time. Say I sit down to write and find myself up against writer's block. If all I can draw on for writing is my "writer" identity, I am in trouble. But if I see my various identities as neighbors instead of as separate houses, I can call on my persona as a priest, for example, to help me. As a priest, I often help people to overcome their blocks.

Perhaps I'm trying to write an article about the Grand Tetons and am at a loss for words. The priest thinks of cathedrals in stone, uniting earth to God and heaven to earth. The cat parent might see the clouds about the mountains as coming "on little cats' feet," as e.e. cummings put it. The cook might see the Tetons as giant bubbles in the boiling stewpot of creation. Suddenly, the writer's block is gone and the pen is flowing happily again.

Polyphrenia is the hallmark of the sentimental mind, for there the complexity of the heart and the multifaceted diversity of the mind become as one. How many of our blocks might be removed if we were sentimental in just this way— as parents, as teachers, as men and women of business, as peacemakers, or as sick people looking to be healed?

∞

The polyphrenic sentimental mind carries within itself an invitation to go beyond, to something more. That metaphrenic place is what I call the soul. Here we are invited to transcend our identities and come to the core.

The story of Jesus is a powerful lesson in what happens to someone who goes beyond his heart and mind without losing the gist of them. Jesus said that "the Kingdom of God is within you,"(Luke 17:21) but the story of what that meant to him remains generally untold. To tell it, let's look at the different ways in which people came to know Jesus.

The first, we might call biographical—details that those who believe in Jesus see as important facts about his life. Jesus was the Son of God, born to the Virgin Mary, who conceived him by the Holy Spirit. His foster father was Joseph, the carpenter of Nazareth. His relatives included Elizabeth and John the Baptist. He was born in Bethlehem and lived with his family in Nazareth until he was about thirty. Then he began a public life of preaching, teaching, and healing, which resulted in strident opposition and ultimately in his crucifixion. He rose from the dead three days later and ascended into heaven forty days after that. Roughly speaking, those are the biographical details of Jesus' life.

But there is another story of Jesus—the story of his works. The gospels are full of these stories. His miracles are legion—curing Simon's mother-in-law, healing the man with the withered hand, curing the paralyzed man whose friends lowered him through the roof, multiplying the loaves and the fishes, turning water to wine at Cana, and so on. His parables are legend—the parable of the sower, the prodigal son, the birds of the air, the widow's mite. His teachings transcend time—the Sermon on the Mount, the two great commandments, the necessity of leaving all things in order to

find out what is most important. People clamored for Jesus'
words and works, so much so that he had to remind them
that he was not there just to do miracles.

A higher purpose comes from the third way of telling
Jesus' story. It comes not primarily from something others
say about Jesus or remember about him; rather it comes from
what amounts to a personal revelation by Jesus to others
about an identity that transcended his biography and his
accomplishments. We see this innermost level of Jesus man-
ifested in the "I am" statements in the Gospel of John. When
Jesus says, "I am the bread of life," "I am the resurrection and
the life," "I am the good shepherd," "I am the vine and my
Father is the vinedresser," "I am the vine and you are the
branches," "I am the door of the sheepgate," and so on, he is
revealing an aspect of himself that is simply not covered in his
biography or his list of accomplishments. His followers find
in these statements an inner energy and identity that fuel his
biographical details and his many achievements. They find
themselves getting a glimpse into the soul of Jesus, and they
feel that they are looking into the soul of God.

Reading these I-statements of Jesus, I am reminded of the
day when as a young man I was talking to my mother about
marriage. Out of the blue, Mom revealed her secret, a wisdom I had not learned from knowing the details of her life
or from her achievements or possessions. "The secret of a
good marriage," Mom confided, "is for the husband and wife
to grow together." There was a moment of revelation. Some-

thing similar happened the first time I interviewed Steve Allen on "As You Think." It was a telephone interview, and Steve was in his son's house in California. At the end of the interview, I asked what was his favorite among his many accomplishments.

"Father, I'm doing it right now," he replied without a moment's hesitation. I'm sitting here rocking my little grand-daughter Amanda."

As my Jewish friends say, now there's a *mensch*!

The sentimental soul—the place of true and lasting identity—is what keeps the sentimental heart and the sentimental mind from being as mushy as our society tends to think they are. There is a place, inner, beyond, but profoundly accessible, that makes them solid and real and strong.

For in the final analysis, it's not your family name or professional affiliations that make you. Bright reputations are smashed to smithereens every day. Neither is it your trophies and achievements. How quickly they are forgotten.

It is the sentimental soul—that inner place of truth about what matters most—that, when discovered, fuels the others and becomes the true benchmark of who you are. Dad was right—it is a virtue, not a weakness, to be sentimental. In these complicated times, when our lives can be so complex, being sentimental of mind, heart, and soul enables us to navigate life's choppy seas with inner calm.

CHAPTER SIX

Hearts, Cores, and Apples

Nature has a powerful way of opening the human heart, of soothing it when it is anxious and healing it when it is down or vulnerable. That is because we are part of nature. Often we speak as though nature were something entirely outside of us. Yet the air, the plants, and the animals are given to us precisely because we are meant not only to use them appropriately, but to help them fulfill God's purpose for their being on earth. Treat a plant or an animal with kindness, and you will watch it transform itself from something ordinary into something radiantly beautiful, an image of God.

Heartstorming—the process of discovering what is in our hearts and the ways in which our hearts can enhance us—is first and foremost a work of nature. The heart is a natural thing, performing a natural function in our bodies—nourishing and cleansing every part of them. Do our emotional hearts have a similar function in our growth toward fulfilling our destiny? Do they center the flow of life just as our physical hearts do for our bodies?

The process of heartstorming has an amazing capacity to do magic. Once we begin to focus on the heart, to observe and to muse about its contents, an amazing array of things present themselves to our awareness. Events we haven't thought about for years suddenly reappear for us to treasure as memories, but also to look at in new ways. It tells us that the heart is a magical kingdom. Its meat and drink are surprise and the unexpected. It sees familiar things in new and interesting ways.

Musing on my heart one day, in this odd process of jumpstarting it again, I suddenly remembered Apple Day. I hadn't thought of Apple Day in years. It was always a Saturday, and it was the day kids went from door to door selling bright Red Delicious apples for charity. It was a day that made a boy like me aware of apples—their deep red outer skin shone with a bright polish that warmed my heart. I recall having mixed feelings: on the one hand, I couldn't wait to bite into one; but on the other hand, biting meant destroying the outer beauty. Seldom did I hesitate for long, however, to savor the sweet yet pungent delight that awaited my sturdy young teeth and active taste buds. Never was I disappointed, and to this day I can recall the wonderful sensation of taste and smell that burst forth once I decided to sink my teeth into it.

Beneath the sweet meat of the apple, there lay a core—a hard center, tough and not so sweet, that contained seeds. If you swallowed the core, it might stick in your throat, and who wanted to swallow the tiny seeds? They, too, could make you choke, and their hardness was impenetrable and uncomfortable to the teeth. The core was useless to a young apple consumer like me, a thing to be cut out and thrown away.

I did not know then, but learned later, that the English word *core* derives from the Latin word *cor*, meaning "heart." That useless appendage that I so quickly discounted and disposed of was the *heart* of the apple.

∽

Reflecting on this long after my boyhood run of Apple Days had gone, I realized that we eat apples the way we do so many other things in life—rushing to get what we want and ignoring the core, the heart of things.

There are so many wonderful things about an apple. One of them, which we barely notice, is its perfume. Once again, we are tempted to use the word *bouquet* for the smell of an apple because it has the essence of a bouquet of flowers. Pick up an apple, and take a moment to smell it before biting into it. The smell of an apple is the threshold that unlocks the secrets, the mysteries that lie within. Accustom yourself to this olfactory moment every time you pick up an apple. You'll discover something wonderful. After a while, you'll discover that each type of apple has its own unique smell, just as it has its own unique taste. We think of *tasting* a Delicious, a Jonathan, and a Macintosh—why do we never think of distinguishing them by their smell? Once you make smelling the apple a ritual, you will never perceive apples in quite the same way again. Just as the scent of another person is the gateway to experiencing him or her, so it is for an apple. That sweet, mouthwatering perfume is there to lure us, to tantalize us, to hypnotize us, if you will. It is God's way of telling us to be ready for mystery and delight.

After experiencing the bouquet of the apple and enjoying the beauty of its red (or green or yellow) skin, it is not yet time to bite in. It's time to allow the feel of the apple to work its magic on you. There is nothing quite so comforting as the smooth texture of an apple's skin. When the road of life becomes bumpy and the affairs of our lives beat us up, the smoothness of the apple is comforting to the touch and to the heart. There is a coolness to the outside of the apple that can calm us. Gently rub your fingers along the apple's surface and allow it to center you, to steady you, to calm you. It's not only that the apple itself is comforting to the touch. It's also that the mere exercise of taking time to feel the apple and to be transformed by its smoothness is itself a calming meditation. When we say we don't have time to pray, maybe all we need to enter the heavenly kingdom is a Jonathan to hold in our hand. Is that what Jesus meant when he told us "the kingdom of heaven is at hand"?

Now, it's time to bite, but wait—don't let your attention turn to the taste just yet, for there's one more key to the mystery of the outer apple to enjoy. Did you hear that crunch? I once had a telephone friend whose kitchen had a squeaky door. That door was the main entrance to the house; whenever anyone entered or left the house, you could hear the hinges squeak to announce the arrival or the departure. The crunch of the apple is just like that. It is the creaking of the hinges of the doorway to the realm within. Don't miss that sound: it is the apple's way of greeting you as it welcomes you into its inner secrets.

Once in the door, we can turn our attention to the taste. The sweetness of the apple is a delight to our taste buds. Each species of apple does it differently. In fact, some apples, better for cooking, are not sweet at all but in their sourness invite a whole realm of creative possibilities—pies, cakes, tarts, strudels, brown bettys, and on and on. As we enjoy the taste of the apple, we find ourselves invited into its deepest core. Inside the apple, we see the pure white hue of the fruit. White is the color of purity, of holiness, and of joy. No wonder the popular derivations of the story of Adam and Eve see the apple as the hinge upon which turned our first parents' decision about the fundamental orientation of the rest of their lives—and ours. How sad, though, that the apple has wrongly taken the blame for their downfall.

At last we come to the core, the heart of the apple, which holds it together and gives it a center. The core is harder than the rest of the apple, and it has to be. For in addition to centering the apple, it holds the seeds. These are the apple's future, and the core holds them with care. At the same time, the core must take under its wing the past, the present, and the future of the apple. The apple came from seeds, the core holds it together in its present state, and now it holds the seeds that herald the future. Don't eat the core of the apple, for it might stick in your throat. Like a mother cat protecting her kittens, the core will do violence to you if you harm its young.

In assessing the apple, let's not forget the stem. It once connected the apple to the tree it came from. Now it serves as a banner proclaiming its proud function as the apple's link to life and drawing attention to the various delights the apple holds in store.

Just as the core is at the center of the apple, the heart is at our center. It is what holds us together and gives us a center. Often, we go after the beauty and the taste and completely miss the heart—the core—which seems so unimportant when we are savoring the moment. The heart holds all our feelings together, even when they are at war with one another. The heart holds them all together, just letting them be.

∞

As the core does for the apple, the heart unifies the various aspects of each individual. Without the core of the apple, the skin and the meat would lose their beauty, would lack coherence. We would have no way of knowing them, much less of appreciating and enjoying them.

So many times, our lives seem to lack coherence. One night on a train, I got into a conversation with a highly successful businessman exhausted from a grueling work week. The tired young man was going home to an equally grueling weekend of athletic events and practices for his kids, all of whom were heavily involved in sports. He was a good man, and I knew that sooner or later he would take time for his own heart. But at that moment, his life felt like a treadmill of perpetual activity. For the moment, he had lost touch with his core, and was just getting through the round of obligations. Many of us, though, do not break through the rat race to any inner core. We wonder why the status, the possessions, the jobs we once found so attractive, deplete us rather than bring us the happiness we thought they had promised. As the saying goes, we lose heart.

The apple core holds seeds, which are the future of the apple, the contribution it makes to the next generation. In the same way, the heart holds the seeds of our future, the ways in which the feelings and impressions of the past and present become the seeds of continuity and creativity for our lives. The heart is the treasure chest of the imaginative life. As you think in your heart, so shall you be, the Bible tells us.

The core of an apple is difficult to chew, and can stick in the throat. By the same token, the human heart is not meant to be devoured or consumed, despite the best efforts of manufacturers and advertisers to convince us that we can win someone's heart with presents. Like the core of the apple, the heart can stick in the throat that tries to turn it into a commodity. When we treasure things that are mere stepping-stones to power, prestige, or some other superficial goal, our core can become hard and mercenary. As it turns toward feelings such as greed, envy, covetousness, and lust, the heart becomes constricted and has less time for noble feelings such as love, joy, satisfaction, care, gratitude, and mercy. The ambience of the heart becomes negative and grasping, rather than positive and open. Tuned into a consumer force, which it was never meant to be, the heart sticks in the throat, chokes us, and defeats the purposes of integrity and joy for which it was intended.

∞

I am unable to look at an apple without thinking of the heart. There are many parallels between the two. The apple, in fact, is shaped somewhat like a heart, though more truly round. Hearts and apples have the same symmetry—two well-defined sides and a center. Many apples (not all, of course) are red—the color of love usually associated with the heart. Like hearts, apples have veins.

Etymologically, the core of the apple is an important icon for understanding the heart. Just as the core is the center of the apple, so the heart is the center of the person. Though the heart is not precisely at the center of the body, it is very much the center of the inner life. We pledge to love someone with all our heart. We place our hand over our heart to salute the flag. Though someone's manner may not be the best, still we say, "His heart is in the right place." When a colleague gives in to circumlocution, we work to get her back to "the heart of the matter." The heart is the core of our being.

It takes a kind of intelligence to hold the various parts of the apple together as the core does. The heart, too, has a certain *savoir faire* by which it holds together so many aspects of our lives. Physically, the pumping of the heart sends fresh blood along the superhighway of the arteries and veins and keeps us alive. Psychologically, the heart provides a home for a vast array of emotions, which often enough are in conflict with one another. It tries to help them coexist in peace. Spiritually, the heart gives guidance and suggestions. How often have you been told to "follow your heart"?

In fact, that guidance provided by the heart is like the seeds held by the apple core. The heart contains the seeds of our future—our dreams and hopes, our fears, our hurts and worries, the joy we hope for both now and in the future. These become implanted in the soil of our daily life and bear fruit in our lives. "The thing I most feared has come upon me," cried our friend Job. A farmer would be thrilled if the seeds in his field bore fruit in the same proportion as the seeds in our heart bear fruit in the field of life.

There is another similarity between the core of an apple and the heart. We noted earlier that one has to be careful not to swallow the core when eating an apple. The core is hard and can stick in the throat.

It may seem strange to speak about swallowing or consuming the heart, but it's something to be careful of nonetheless. There is a difference between consumerism and legitimate consumption. Nonetheless, when the heart becomes materialistic, it is as though the heart itself were being consumed. A heart that is focused exclusively on things is a heart that is living at a lesser level than it was intended to. A heart that is focused on things chokes us after a while. When possessions become our sole focus, we become blocked. Our hearts harden and our spirit gasps for life.

Hearts, cores, and apples have a remarkable similarity. They lead us to the deepest meaning of life.

∞

When apples touch the heart and mind, do they also touch the soul? The Bible tells us that they do. Apples are mentioned seven times in the Hebrew Bible. Four of those references use the expression "the apple of [one's] eye." Sometimes, as in Deuteronomy 32:10, the reference is to God's outstanding love for his people, whom he brought forth from exile: "In a desert land he found him. . . . he guarded him as the apple of his eye."

In Zechariah, the expression is part of a prophecy about the restoration of Jerusalem and how highly the Lord values his people: "Whoever touches you touches the apple of his eye" (2:8).

In Proverbs, the young disciple seeking wisdom is exhorted to "guard my teachings as the apple of your eye" (7:2).

There is a certain eroticism about the apple as referenced in the Song of Solomon. In the second chapter of that mystical poem, the poet refers to the delectability of the apple tree and compares it to the lover: "Like an apple tree among the trees of the forest is my lover among the young men. I delight to sit in his shade, and his fruit is sweet to my taste" (2:3). Later, the apple tree is the scene of erotic union and new life: "Under the apple tree I roused you; there your mother conceived you, there she who was in labor gave you birth" (8:5).

In Joel 1:12, the apple tree is a source of joy for humankind, and the demise of the apple tree causes the joy of the human race to "wither away."

Scripture, then, sees the apple as a sign of favor, a sign of love and procreation, and a sign of joy. The Bible makes a strong connection between apples and God as signs of divine life and creativity and favor.

It's not only the Judeo-Christian scriptures that honor the apple. Some ancient, earth-based religions that worship the divine feminine see the apple as auspicious and sacred, "a symbol of the sacred feminine." And the holy writings of Ba'hai, a universalist religion whose doctrines are rooted in Shiite Islam, also speak of "the apple of the eye." Though someone be of a different faith, if he should believe in the divine, *The World Order of Baha'u'llah* proclaims, "I will regard him as the apple of my eye."

Perhaps that is why God tucked so many secrets into the apple: sense by sense, layer by layer, down to its very core, the apple, like the heart, leads us into the depths of God.

CHAPTER SEVEN

The Cockles of the Heart

I went for years not knowing what a cockle was. Looking back, I suppose I was not a very curious child. Over and over again my mother read to me the nursery rhyme about "Mary, Mary, quite contrary," who in response to inquiries about her horticulture replied, "with silver bells and cockle shells. . . ." Why I didn't wonder about cockle shells, I'll never know. Perhaps, even at a tender age, the "pretty maids all in a row" got the best of me.

Then there was "Alive Alive Ho." The ballad of sweet Molly Malone, who cried "cockles and mussels alive alive ho," should have given me some clue or at least some curiosity, but it didn't. I blissfully sang the lyrics, thinking not at all about what I was singing. Amazing.

My shell of ignorance about cockles began to crack open finally when I heard someone say, "It will warm the cockles of your heart." I suppose they were talking about a poem or a sentiment or even a warm drink on a cold day; I don't recall. But that was the one that got to me. "Cockles of my heart?" I wondered, finally dumbfounded. "I didn't know my heart had cockles." And at last, "What are cockles, anyway?"

To the dictionary I went, only to be even more puzzled. A cockle, I learned, was a mollusk having a shell with "convex radially ribbed valves." There was even a picture of a cockleshell to match the definition. Looking at the etymology of the word *cockle*, I saw it was related to the French word *coquille*, as in *Coquille St. Jacques*, a most appetizing way to serve scallops. Now I was getting somewhere. The dictionary also told me that the word *cockle* could be used as a synonym for the cockleshell. That was another useful piece of information.

But not entirely. I was still puzzled. I didn't have a shell around my heart, at least not as far as I knew. But if I did, how ever would I warm it?

Perhaps, I mused, the expression referred to the structure of the rib cage, which protects the heart the way the shell protects the mollusk and keeps it from being hurt or damaged by a blow or a fall. It can't mean that the heart is a shell, I reasoned. The heart is a soft, tender muscle, with its own strength and resiliency, of course, but with none of the toughness of a shell. Plus, it hardly seems as though the expression could refer to warming the rib cage. How utterly unromantic.

Perhaps the phrase "warm the cockles of your heart" is meant to invite us to picture the heart in a new way. Perhaps it's meant to be a metaphor in which the heart itself is compared to a shell in that it protects the various tender feelings and impressions that it contains. In this scenario, the heart is like a mother hen who sits on the nest, protecting the eggs from being broken or stolen.

Besides protecting them, the mother hen warms the eggs. That's why they hatch and baby chicks are born. When we speak of warming the cockles of the heart, perhaps we are saying that the heart warms the notions and sentiments that are inside it, instilling them with life, vitality, zest. Or again, perhaps the expression is saying that the heart is like an oven. When I bake bread, I mix all the ingredients together and put them into a bread pan and place it all in the oven. The warmth of the oven makes the ingredients warm, then move, then rise and form into a loaf. Beat it down, repeat the process again a couple of times, and you have a new creation—a warm, delicious loaf of bread.

The cockles of the heart warm and protect the feelings and impression the heart holds.

The oyster, the clam, and the mussel provide us with a good image of how the heart protects. Their respective shells are very different, but all serve to protect the delicate creature within. What is especially fascinating is the intricate beauty of the shells. Look closely at the outer shell of a clam or an oyster. Notice the subtle coloring—the more you look at the shell, the more colors you see. And, oh, the intricate patterns! At times they are almost rainbows of blue and gray. Mussel shells have a special beauty, a deep gorgeous ebony whose elegance enchants you. Isn't it strange that shells can have such beauty? We so often underrate them, ignore them, take them for granted, and toss them away as though they were nothing.

One of the joys of my culinary life the past couple of years has been the discovery of clay oven cooking. The first time I saw a clay oven in the store, it was love. The clay oven is a shell that warms. You put your roast or bird or filet of fish into the clay oven. You cover it with carrots, onions, celery, spices, and some wine. Then place the clay cover on top, place in your cold oven, turn the temperature to around 475 degrees, and cook until done. The result is ambrosial. The clay oven takes on the high temperature of your conventional oven, intensifies and protects that temperature, all the while holding in the flavor. The clay oven is the best image I have found to illustrate the cockles of the heart. Like the heart, it warms its contents, protects their flavor, and seasons and matures them all at once.

In some respects, it sounds unflattering to speak of the heart as a shell. We prefer to think of the heart as unfettered and free, and rightly so. In counseling, our tendency is to crack the shells of the people who come to us, to break down their resistance and defenses. When I was in the novitiate of a religious community, the novice master was reported to have pledged to "break" one of the novices who was steadfastly resisting him. He succeeded in his intention, and the man went on to be a successful priest. But the thought of breaking someone else horrified me and made me extremely wary of that man and his system.

I'm not inclined to break people's shells. Instead, I tend to be curious as to why they're there, to see whether in due time they might crack. As we have observed in the mollusk world, there is a natural beauty to some of the shells we create—if we take time to look at them and admire their intricacy. Some shells are remarkable for the sheer labor their makers have in producing them.

Let's call them Matt and Lynn, the wise and loving parents of a little boy we shall call Jack. In infancy, Jack was diagnosed with borderline autism. Pictures from those days reflect little light in Jack's eyes, and as he grew older he withdrew into his own world. Every expert Matt and Lynn consulted wanted to do elaborate testing, all of which ended in the same conclusion: Jack would never have a normal life. Matt and Lynn weren't convinced. It was heartbreaking to see their little boy like this, but after a while they developed a fascination with his behavior. Contrary to the dire predictions of the doctors, they decided to allow Jack to develop at his own pace. They saw him not as a problem, but as a human being struggling to find his way in the world. When I met

Jack as a family friend, I saw the wisdom of his parents'
allowing him to grow at his own pace. When I first came to
his house, Jack ran away to hide. I decided to honor his shyness, and went about my business. In about ten minutes, there
he was running up to me—"Father Paul, it's me, Jack!"
Because I had honored his shell, he felt safe to leave it. That
was the philosophy Matt and Lynn used with Jack, and it
worked wonders. Each step of the way they encouraged him,
honored his reservations, and allowed him to grow at his own
pace. How proud they were when, at age seven, Jack stood
up in front of a crowd of parents and read a twenty-eight-
page story he had written! Who knows what Jack will do or
how far he will go, but it's to his benefit that his parents chose
to be fascinated by his shell, to respect it, and to allow the little person inside to grow at his own pace.

Shells around our hearts can be wonderful things. At
times I put a shell up around myself, place myself physically
and spiritually where few can find me, and completely relax.
Putting up that shell, no matter how antisocial it may seem,
allows me to feel a deep inner peace and gives me time to
read and meditate, to enjoy the beauty of nature, and to feel
like myself again. Years ago, a colleague of mine in the dean's
office of a college told me that when things got really tough,
she would go to the store and buy a huge supply of limburger
cheese, go home, and hole up for the night. Now that's a
shell!

Our shells can mask feelings of inadequacy and shyness, and popular wisdom would tell us that we would be better off breaking out of those shells and healing those "dysfunctional" feelings. What the common wisdom often forgets is that those very shells that it derides often inspire enormous creativity. Emily Dickinson never left her home and often dressed in the fashion of a bygone era; but, oh, how her poetry has touched the hearts of people throughout the world!

Sometimes we put up shells around ourselves in a time of grief. Such shells are necessary for us to survive. When Cardinal O'Connor died, I had to put my feelings on hold for five days and help our office deal with the needs of the media. For days I watched as 150,000 people streamed by the Cardinal's casket in St. Patrick's Cathedral and tens of thousands more filled the church for various services in his memory, including the funeral Mass itself. There was no chance for me to get in line. Finally, on Monday morning, before the funeral, I was waiting inside the cathedral while a press photographer took some pictures. They were closing the cathedral to the public to prepare for the ceremony, and the honor guard attending the Cardinal's casket was moved away. In a flash I saw that the cathedral was nearly empty, that there was no honor guard and no one praying before the Cardinal's coffin. There was my chance. I went up to the communion rail, knelt in front of the Cardinal's body, alone with him as we had been on many wonderful occasions during his life. I was able to thank him for all he had done for me and to pray for the repose of his soul. God provided an invisible shell around me to allow me time to pay my respects.

In the days following the funeral, I found myself putting up a shell around my heart. I found myself turning down interview requests to talk about the Cardinal. Normally, I would have been happy for such opportunities, but I just couldn't talk about the Cardinal. In the office, I was very quiet, just going about my duties with few words and little humor. For the most part, I avoided E-mails. For a solid two or three weeks my heart was heavy with grief. Eventually the shell that protected my tender heart began to crack, and I was able to feel joy again. The shell was no longer needed.

How often we hear of people telling grieving friends and family members, "Snap out of it. Get on with your life." It's important to realize the value of the shell that those who grieve put around themselves. It's a way of protecting their vulnerable hearts until they are well enough to go on again. Though there are things grieving people can do to help themselves as they mourn, the process pretty much takes its own time. It's important for others to honor the shell of grief and not to try to break it down prematurely.

Is there a time when a shell is not a positive thing? A shell is problematic when it is destructive of oneself or others. A person may retreat into silence if hurt by a family member.

That's fine in the short run, and understanding relatives can tolerate it for a while. But if sulky silences become a way of life, there's a problem. Family members need to respectfully address the wounded heart and get it to face its issues.

Addictions are an attempt to put a shell around a wounded or frightened heart. They are harmful because over time the shells thicken incrementally and increasingly overtake the heart. The heart gets to the point where it needs the shell, or thinks it does, in order to function. Unless something is done to intervene, the person becomes more and more alienated from himself and from the outside world.

Abusing others physically or emotionally is yet another shell that needs to be dealt with and eliminated. Abusive people are masking their own vulnerability, in effect taking it out on others—they need to be helped, and under no circumstances should those around them allow themselves to continue to be their victims.

Ongoing victimhood is another negative shell that people use to defend themselves. There are times when we are victims, but when we begin to see ourselves as victims overall, we are retreating into a belief that we are helpless and that we have no responsibility for our situation or for fixing it. The sooner the person breaks through the shell and gains a sense of personal power and responsibility, the better.

Shells can be destructive and negative. But it's important to remember that they can also be temporary ways of coping with the stresses and blows of life. Unless they are destructive, we do well to honor our shells and those of others. Underneath them lies a heart waiting to heal.

∞

Can the shells in our lives lead us to be more soulful? Can they lead us to God? I think the Book of Jonah in the Bible is a great "shell" book, for it is a story of hiding and finding, and a story of how God makes shells for us and even breaks them.

Jonah is a prophet whom God calls to preach against the people of Nineveh, who are steeped in sin and on the verge of being annihilated. It so happens that Jonah hates the Ninevites—the last thing he wants them to do is to repent. So he decides to stow away on a ship bound for the distant seas. Effectively, Jonah uses the ship as a shell to hide himself from God. His strategy works beautifully until a storm at sea threatens to destroy the ship. The sailors come across the stowaway, and when they find out that he is fleeing God, he persuades them to throw him overboard. So much for Jonah's first shell. This time, God creates a shell for his renegade prophet. He arranges for a great fish to swallow Jonah, and the prophet is holed up in the fish's belly for three days—his second shell. The fish has a double purpose. One, it protects Jonah from the raging seas. Two, it enables Jonah to have plenty of time to think about what he is doing. Jonah composes a long prayer of repentance, at the end of which he promises to do God's bidding. So God allows the fish to spew him forth onto the shore. Jonah then goes to Nineveh and indeed does God's bidding. He prophesies so well that the people repent in an instant and God pardons them.

Jonah is so angry with God over the repentance of the Ninevites and his forgiveness of them that he rebukes God. He tells God to let him die—a rather extreme reaction to his unwanted success. Sulking, he goes to a place east of the city and builds himself a shelter were he can sit and sulk—his third shell. Now God provides Jonah's fourth shell—a castor-oil plant to shade Jonah from the hot sun and to improve his humor. It worked; Jonah was delighted with the plant.

But the next morning, God arranges for the elements to destroy the plant, and once again God finds Jonah praying for death in the heat of the sun. God talks to Jonah and asks how the prophet could be so attached to something (the plant) that he did not make, yet fail to understand how God could be so concerned for a people he did make—the Ninevites. By so addressing Jonah, God tries to help him to remove another shell—the most important one—the shell of racism around his heart. That is the shell that drives the story from beginning to end.

In its relentless effort to help us to find our purpose on earth, the soul, like God in the Jonah story, may sometimes erect shells and sometimes tear them down. Both the erecting and the tearing down are the soul's way of showing us that the best way to live is to live deeply, to live in a sense of divine direction and love.

There is a lesson here, a lesson about the shells we build around our hearts. When we build a shell of hatred or wickedness around our hearts, like Jonah, we end up running from God. This necessitates our building up more shells to defend the first one, and God then has to break them down or build new ones to help us in our weakened condition.

We create shells for a variety of reasons, often to protect our wounded hearts. God works with us and we can work with him and with each other to honor our shells, but in the end to break free of them and find freedom of heart.

CHAPTER EIGHT

Hearts Made of Stone

How to Soften a Hardened Heart

"She shall not live; no, my heart is turned to stone; I strike it, and it hurts my hand." Shakespeare's Othello tells us pithily what happens when our hearts turn to stone. When our hearts turn hard and cold and murderous, it matters not if our intended victim be one like Desdemona, whom "the world hath not a sweeter creature." Amazingly, our hearts can recognize the sweetness, but still want to destroy it.

I've seen those hearts of stone and marveled at how cold they feel. I remember one Friday night taking a commuter train out to a meeting. When we reached the station, I left the train and waited in the parking lot for my ride. A young woman in her late twenties was also waiting for someone. Her face darkened with impatience as minute after minute went by. At last, a car pulled up—the driver, I presume, was her husband. She opened the car door and as she got into the car gave him the dirtiest look I have ever seen. Not a word passed between them as she slammed the door and they drove off in deafening silence.

The metaphor of stone is so appropriate for the heart that has become hardened. A stone cannot move itself, and the heart that has become cold and hate-filled can do very little to move itself to another state of being. We speak of people who cannot get out of their own way, and that is true of hard-hearted people.

When we speak of hearts that are made of stone, we're generally thinking of boulders rather than pebbles. Hearts become either loving or hateful over time, and hearts made of stone tend to feel huge because they have taken one or more of the events of life and enlarged it. Years ago, I read a book called *Images of Hope* by William Lynch, which said that we lose hope when we make things bigger than they are. That's right—life appears hopeless when we feel over-whelmed, when life feels so much bigger than we are. Stony hearts got that way because life became so big, so mean, that coldness and hardness became the only response to a world that has treated them badly. The heart feels heavy like a rock, without light or levity.

Hearts that have turned to stone tend to stay that way, resisting every impulse of love that comes their way. In that sense, too, they are rocklike—adamant, we say. They resist everything that is thrown at them. No way are they going to break.

∞

Whether it be permanent or temporary, hardness of heart is one of the worst maladies that can befall a human being. It drains all the color from life and makes everything feel gray and hard.

Why do we let our hearts harden? Usually we don't mean to. With rare exceptions, hard-hearted people don't get that way by choice. It happens after a thousand experiences, a host of decisions as to how to respond to people, and finally one more choice sends one across the line into hardness of heart.

Hearts made of stone are different from hearts with shells. There, the heart is protected and continues to beat normally. Here, the heartbeat is heavy and morose, because the heart has turned to stone.

It's relatively easy to see shells around hearts. It's a little more difficult to determine with certainty whether a heart still continues to beat. It is possible, though, to see when a negative pattern has headed in a wrong direction. During a time of transition in an organization of which he was a member, someone I know only by his screen name took to E-mailing me, fiercely berating the incoming head of his organization. I suggested to him that, though it was fine to have misgivings, it was part of wisdom to give the new man a chance. In return, I received yet another E-mail once again berating the new leader and summoning all sorts of reasons why the writer and others knew that the new man would be a disaster. There was so much venom in the letter that I strongly suspected the writer of having a truly hardened heart, not only on this matter but in general.

Hardness of heart is not the same as courage. I have met battle-scarred military people whose toughness and gruff manner are the result of long and dangerous campaigns, but who have somehow retained a warmth and sensitivity to others beneath their gruff exterior. I have had strong disagreements with people who, like me, heatedly defend their point of view. Yet at the same time we have acknowledged the disagreement and have shaken hands in respect for each other's passion and conviction.

I think hardness of heart happens when one develops the need to be right at all costs. That's when marriages break down, friends become enemies, and violence rules the day. Hardness of heart stems from the failure to realize that no matter who you are or how strong your conviction, there is always another point of view. We put blinders on our hearts when we fail to realize that in being right, we can make ourselves very wrong.

I see the results of the need to be right in families. Husbands and wives come to counseling fighting about money, the children, sex, and a host of other things, each one of them insisting that they are right and their spouse is wrong. Children and parents do the same thing. It takes a great deal of patient endurance to get them to see that there is another point of view and that it is possible to disagree without being hateful.

When we're "right" to the exclusion of everyone else's opinion, we miss a lot. In the movie *Home Alone* there is a subplot about an old man whom everyone in the neighborhood "knows" to be cruel. As the plot unfolds he turns out to be very nice, but is troubled because of a disagreement with his son, with whom he has not spoken in a long time. He would attend his granddaughter's recitals and sit in the back, but never approach her or the family. That gulf is what has been eating away at the man and making him miserable. His hardness of heart—and his son's—have caused both of them to miss the opportunity of knowing each other.

The price of being right in terms of being self-righteous is a high price to pay. We can believe in our position, defend it, and think it reasonable, but to let our rightness consume us is a terrible mistake. It is not worth the string of heartaches and broken relationships that can result.

∞

The soul's response to a heart made of stone and caught in its own rectitude is to urge compassion and forgiveness. They are the drops of rain that, falling upon the stony heart, will gradually erode it and replace it with a heart of flesh.

Compassion is literally the ability to suffer with someone. When we think that someone has done us wrong, we believe that we suffer while the one who hurt us does not. We further believe that this situation is grossly unfair. When we seek revenge, we do so because we believe that the other person will suffer and we, at last, will rejoice. Compassion means suffering with the other person, realizing that anyone who would do such a terrible thing must have considerable pain inside. We might seriously ask ourselves, "Why in the world would someone do something like that to me?" We may not get answers exactly, but we might just get a clue or a glimmer of an idea. Maybe the person was desperate. Maybe she misunderstood something that was said, or she was given some wrong information by someone else. Maybe he is angry in general, and we realize what a miserable way that is to go through life and feel sorry for him. Compassion—suffering with the other person—may not soothe our feelings entirely, but it can break the hardness of them by giving us a different perspective.

Compassion can lead to forgiveness. When our hearts have been hardened by someone's wrongdoing, we can take the step of releasing the matter entirely and setting our hearts free. There is a general misunderstanding about the nature of forgiveness. We are often afraid to forgive because we find it distasteful to do something that will benefit the other person—let them off the hook, so to speak. The thing is, forgiveness may or may not benefit the one being forgiven, but it will most certainly benefit the one forgiving. It is amazing how much better you feel when you let your heart lighten. It's better for your physical health, too. Holding grudges blocks our ability to heal and makes us more susceptible to illness. Forgiveness frees us.

A more fundamental misunderstanding of the nature of forgiveness leads us to confuse forgiveness and reconciliation. We often say that we can't forgive until the other person calls us and apologizes. It's not true. Regardless of whether the offending party apologizes, we can let go of the incident, release our feelings, and be free. Or we can hold on to them and let them fossilize us.

Is forgiveness really letting the other person off the hook as it seems? Forgiving people does not mean you validate their actions. It does not diminish an offender's responsibility to make restitution for any damage done. It does not give anyone permission to hurt us again. For forgiveness is really about healing ourselves and hoping that the other person will experience a change of heart for her own good.

True forgiveness takes us down to a deep level of the soul. It helps us to get past the chains that bind us to our own hurts, but also frees us from encasing our hearts in chains over what we expect or require of others. Once we have experienced God's inner peace it is no long quite so important whether someone else does something or not. Our concerns take an entirely different direction. We want peace and we want to be peacemakers. We no longer want—or have—hearts made of stone.

Not long ago, I experienced a poignant example of the ways in which the soul can jostle us to the freedom that forgiveness can bring. At the funeral of a close friend, I happened to run into a colleague who was also close to the deceased. Over the years, the relationship between the colleague and me had, for a host of reasons too petty to remember, turned to stone. To his eternal credit, the man said to me, "You know, I think it would make our friend happy if you and I got along better. Let's make that part of his legacy." Immediately, I felt the hardness in my heart melt away, replaced by harmony and love.

The soul does things like that. It lobbies, almost despite us, for healing and reconciliation. Like Othello, our hearts can become so hardened that we could break our hand on them. Our soul keeps sending grace, like water, drop by drop upon the rock, wearing it down until all that is left are a bright soul, a compassionate mind, and a gentle heart.

CHAPTER NINE

The Heart Has Its Reasons

It was Valentine's Day, 1988, and I was living in the Bronx in a Jesuit house on Belmont Street called Ciszek Hall. It was early in the evening, and I was sitting downstairs watching television when I was told I had a phone call. It was my father calling from Missouri. I had just spoken to Dad for his birthday two days earlier, and was surprised to hear from him again so soon. I loved Dad, and knew he was dealing bravely with the loss of Mom almost three years before. I was a little bit on edge with his call. Dad could be critical at times and I wasn't sure whether this call had an agenda. Strangely, he didn't seem to have much to say. There were pauses and breaks in the conversation and the whole thing didn't seem to be headed anywhere. After I hung up the phone, I shook my head. *What was* that *all about?*

About two weeks later, on a Saturday morning around seven o'clock, I was eating breakfast at Mount Manresa Retreat House on Staten Island. I was looking forward to helping with a parish mission later that night, but one phone call changed all that. Father Thomas from Missouri called me to say that Dad had died that very morning in an airport limousine, apparently of a heart attack. He had left his apartment five minutes before and was heading to the airport for a trip to San Diego.

As I struggled to put my thoughts together in the days that followed, that Valentine's Day phone call from Dad kept coming back to me. It had seemed so rambling and pointless, so unlike other conversations with Dad. I kept wondering, was it possible that Dad had had a premonition that he was about to die?

When I got to Missouri and entered Dad's apartment, my sense was that he had arranged everything for me. There was the birthday card I had sent him just days before, sitting on the television. His tax documents were out on the kitchen table where he had been working on them before he left. Ever the early bird, he had been getting ready to file. Also on hand was his address book with the name of his lawyer. Everything I needed was there when I needed it.

The more I thought about it, the more I realized that all of this had not happened by accident. I came to understand that Dad's mysterious Valentine's Day call came from his inner premonition that he was going to die. He had prepared everything for me because, at some level, he knew I would need it.

Dad gave me a valuable lesson in the heart's way of knowing. His death was from a myocardial infarction, and was entirely due to natural causes. He had never complained of symptoms or any discomfort. Yet somehow he knew his time had come.

The other piece of the story is that Dad listened to what his heart told him and acted on it. Many of us brush off the intimations of our hearts, but Dad didn't. What makes this fact more remarkable is that this was *Dad*. Though a deeply loving and devoted man, he was the one who once told me, "Any time you make a decision, be sure that you make it completely rationally. Always keep your feelings out of it." Somewhere along the way, Dad had learned to put his heart into the mix.

"The heart has its reasons which reason knows not of"— Pascal was right. The heart gives us premonitions, such as Dad's. It can also help us to read between the lines. Our hearts can tell us when something about a business deal seems to be wrong. We can't put our finger on it, but something's not quite right. Our hearts can tell us when someone is lying to us. We just know. If we listen to our heart, we can then go to our mind to figure out what is wrong, and to our soul for God's guidance on what to do about it.

On my radio program "As You Think," I close each show with a little variation on a verse from the Book of Proverbs.

I say, "As you think in your heart, so shall you be" (23:7). The thoughts of our minds are important, but they are colored by the thoughts of our hearts. Advertisers know this. When they want us to try their products, they put something on the screen that will give us a good feeling and a positive association with it. From there we decide to buy the product.

∞

What kind of knowledge is the knowledge of the heart? We often speak as though such knowings are hunches, but that doesn't really do justice to what the heart knows. In fact, the heart's knowledge runs along the lines of certain general principles.

1. Certain things are good for us and others are not. The heart guides us toward what we believe to be good for us and away from what we believe will be harmful to us.

2. We are happiest when we revere ourselves and others, and when others revere us.

3. We can love ourselves even when we disappoint ourselves.

4. Our negative feelings can be signs that we need to change certain things in our lives.

5. Beyond our individual feelings and impressions, there is an overall sense of mission or purpose in life that is available to us.

Let's look at each of these.

1. **Certain things are good for us and others are not. The heart guides us toward what we believe to be good for us and away from what we believe will be harmful to us.** St. Augustine wrote, "My love is my weight," meaning that our love draws us in certain directions. My almost inborn love for radio reflects my heart's belief that I would do well to be involved in the radio world in some way. Not long ago, I happened to meet a young woman who has a passionate interest in art deco radios, those antique plastic radios whose design lends style and warm sound to the instrument. Her passion for them knows no bounds and has led her to be both an avid collector of them and a writer.

On the other side of the fence, the heart can steer us away from what it perceives as danger. A friend counsels people who are in a strange neighborhood to listen to their feelings when walking in the area. If they feel a strong sense of foreboding, she says, it would be wise to heed those feelings and alter their course.

There's a question of discernment here, though. We all have had feelings of fear when facing a new experience or a risk. We also know that sometimes it is just not smart to give in to our fears. What to do? The first day of broadcasting school, I was so scared I could hardly get myself to cross the threshold into the classroom. I found myself saying, "I don't need to do this. I'll be fine if I forget about broadcasting. It's not important anyway. Why don't I just go home?" Fortunately, I didn't give in to those fears. I crossed the threshold, and, as it turned out, walked into a whole new phase of my life.

These sorts of feelings signal danger. They're good, because they tell us we're moving out of our comfort zone. They tell us that there is a risk. When should we give in to those feelings? There are a few guiding criteria.

Is what I am about to do immoral? If I am scared because I am about to do something that is morally wrong, I am getting a significant piece of information from my heart and I should definitely plan on changing course.

Is what I am about to do going to significantly hurt myself or others? If so, is there a substantially higher benefit that is my real goal and that will offset the harm done? If I am scared to save someone else's life because I am going to die, that's one thing. But if I am reluctant or afraid to say something to someone because in my heart I feel that this may not be a good time to do it, that's entirely different. Perhaps I should follow my heart's lead and wait. There are times when my heart is really ready to blast someone. My discomfort may be a signal that I am about to be hurtful. Take a deep breath, count to ten, and wait.

If it's not immoral or hurtful, what am I afraid of? Am I afraid of change, or is there more to it than that? If I'm still picking up resistance, is it just that I am afraid of change? (That's what I discovered it was when I hesitated at the broadcasting school.) If it seems like more than that, it's a good idea to wait a while. Sometimes the reasons of the heart are so subtle that they warn us of dangers we would not otherwise be aware of, and that will come to light later on.

Those criteria can guide us to discern why our hearts are giving us a panic signal. What else can our heart tell us in this very special knowing it has?

2. We are happiest when we revere ourselves and others, and when others revere us. Though a lot of the advertising we see and hear tries to make us believe that happiness lies in what we possess, our hearts know better. There is a reason that our hearts have a built-in rhythm of giving and receiving. They pump blood out through the arteries and receive it back through the veins. The balance of giving and receiving is the natural rhythm of the heart's flow.

It's true spiritually, too. The heart is at its best when it both gives and receives. When we spend an excessive amount of time giving to others, we experience exhaustion and burnout. On the other hand, when we spend an excessive amount of time receiving and worrying about receiving, we end up self-centered and miserly. It's when we give and receive, with the focus on showing reverence and respect for ourselves and for others, that our hearts become balanced and happy.

3. We can love ourselves even when we disappoint ourselves. "You should be ashamed of yourself." Eliminating that sentence from the language—any language—would be a step in the right direction. There is such a thing as legitimate guilt when we have done something truly wrong, but the hope should always be that the guilt be accompanied by a healthy self-love. Intuitively, the heart knows the difference between ego and who we really are. Guilt has a great deal to do with ego—a person can spend considerable time focusing on how inept he is. What it amounts to is an ego trip. Instead, when we love ourselves, we can acknowledge our sinfulness and our capacity for mistakes yet also acknowledge that this is only a small part of who we are, by no means the entire picture. This enables us to move on and even to learn from our mistakes and to let them lead us into better directions.

4. Our negative feelings can be signs that we need to change certain things in our lives. When we are feeling consistently negative for a considerable period of time, we can feel stuck in those emotions. Instead, we can look at our feelings as guides that tell us that it is time for a change. It may be an actual change of residence or job. Or it may be an inner change that will occasion other changes. When people feel stuck in their marriage, for example, they either hunt for a new mate or (preferably) look within to find out what they might do to restore their marriage. Their feelings are a catalyst for them to get moving.

5. Beyond our individual feelings and impressions, there is an overall sense of a mission and purpose in life that is available to us. German theologian Dietrich Bonhoeffer, in one of his letters from a Nazi prison camp, pointed out that there is a point-counterpoint rhythm to our lives. There are all the events, and then there is the underlying theme. It takes a certain amount of maturation for us to feel the underlying theme of our lives, but it is something to look for and to work toward. We can cultivate it by starting with the premise that we are here to be of service to others, and let our sense specify itself from there. As we begin to cluster our life experiences around the concept of service, we will be led to the particular areas of service that are ours.

The heart knows many things, and by remembering those general principles of its knowledge, we can become increasingly appreciative of its intelligence.

∞

What is the relationship between the reasons of the heart and the life of the soul? As the soul and the heart work closely together and become accustomed to being in tandem, there develops a sense that the guidance of the heart has something to do with God.

To illustrate what this means, consider the biblical story of Naomi and Ruth, found in the first chapter of the Book of Ruth. Having lost her husband and two grown sons, Naomi advises her daughters-in-law to return to their homeland of Moab. One, named Orpah, chose to return home. Ruth, who also had every reason to return, chose not to do so out of love and respect for Naomi. Her words to Naomi are famous: "Where you go I will go, and where you stay I will stay. Your people will be my people and your God my God. . . . May the LORD deal with me, be it ever so severely, if anything but death separates you and me" (1:16–17).

In that moment of decision, Ruth discovered the reasons of her heart, a life purpose that went beyond obligation, even beyond being nice, and that instead went all the way to God. Her act eventually led her to marrying a man named Boaz. Ruth didn't know what would be the outcome of her actions. She said yes to her heart, said yes to God, and let the rest flow forth.

So when I think back to that Valentine's Day and to Dad's phone call, I am grateful that he had learned to follow his heart. Grateful, too, that he took time to share his heart with me. Once again, Dad proved a powerful teacher. He showed me that the heart can be a doorway to God.

CHAPTER TEN

Sacred Hearts

Burning with Love, Crowned with Thorns

As a Catholic boy, my favorite among the statues and holy pictures displayed so prominently in our home was the image of the Sacred Heart of Jesus. The image of Jesus, his piercing eyes so composed and his heart so radiant with love, has touched the hearts of countless Christians throughout the centuries. I was well into adulthood, though, when I discovered the great secret of the Sacred Heart. I realized that at the same time that the divine heart is so radiant with love, a crown of thorns surrounds it. People often ask me about God's role in the various forms of evil and tragedy that are rampant in the world. I always think of the image of the Sacred Heart when I reply that God's heart is wounded by those events, and yet his heart keeps beating with every form of love and assistance at its disposal.

There is something infinitely precious about a heart that suffers and yet keeps beating with love. I have found it in mothers who are deeply hurt by the cruelty and insensitivity of their children, and manage to love them nonetheless. I have seen it in husbands and wives who find the courage and strength to forgive themselves and each other after a betrayal, and go on to deepen their married love. It appears in the bewildered eyes of a young widow who wonders how life could have dealt her so tragic a blow, yet summons the strength to go on.

Sacred hearts are hearts that we hold dear because they have allowed sorrow to refine them. The sacred hearts are those with whom we have shared some affinity in pain. Compassion is the bond that forms when, literally, we "suffer with" someone.

When I was a young priest working as a hospital chaplain, I was privileged to meet and observe many wonderful physicians. The man I will call Dr. Jackson was my favorite. Physically, and in his ardent dedication, he reminded me of the wonderful family doctor whose visits to my sickbed saw me through so many childhood illnesses. I came to know Dr. Jackson because he was at Mass every morning before making his rounds. He loved to critique—I should say *criticize*—my homilies. "A little better than yesterday's, Father Keenan," he would tell me. "But you still have a long way to go."

I loved Dr. Jackson both for his compassion and for his learning. Medicine, to him, was a science, but it was also a way of life—it was literature, it was philosophy, it was ethics, it was art, and it was love. He could not resist being my mentor, nor could I resist being his pupil.

"What do you know about Sir William Osler, Father Keenan?" he demanded shortly after we met.

"Not much," I had to admit.

Out from his library appeared a volume of the revered Canadian physician's talks to doctors. I devoured the essays, which showed me so clearly where this mentor of mine received his deep wisdom. Suddenly, I was transported to the great Osler's lecture hall. There I sat among the young physicians, fixated, learning with them about healing and life, hearing the master explain the importance of the human touch in the healing of patients.

I have many fond memories of Dr. Jackson. Indeed, he etched himself permanently into my heart. There is one memory I will never forget—one that taught me so much about sacred hearts and the heart of the physician I had come to revere. I was invited one Sunday evening to the Jackson home for dinner. I don't recall much about the house, except that it had the elegance one would expect from such a charming man. Mrs. Jackson was a lovely woman who set a beautiful table for us. What was astonishing, in the midst of such grace and charm, was a persistent banging noise that came from the back of the house, punctuated by sounds of someone yelling. Without a trace of apology, Dr. Jackson told me, "That's my son." When it came time for us to be seated in the dining room for dinner, the little boy—clearly developmentally disabled—was brought in to sit at the table with us. It was obvious that he had his own abilities and his own world. It was also clear from the demeanor of his parents that this little boy was unconditionally and unabashedly cared for and loved. He was, to them, a sacred heart.

I am sure, though he never said so, that Dr. Jackson would have wanted a son who followed in his footsteps, who shared his love of medicine and philosophy and culture—a kindred soul to commiserate with at the end of a long day of clinic and rounds. That didn't happen. Nonetheless, he remained deeply and obviously devoted to his son and to his patients. Whatever heartache and disappointment there might have been over his son's condition made him a more loving and compassionate parent and physician. Whatever pain was in his heart, that heart burned with love. Dr. Jackson, too, was a sacred heart.

These are sacred hearts. A bond of suffering and love binds them to us. Like Christ in the picture, they transfix us and lift us up. We understand them with a love that may boggle the mind, but that touches the understanding of the heart.

I have thought about Dr. Jackson many times over the years since I last saw him. I have often wondered what enabled people like him and his wife to love so deeply and intensely, and whether there was something all of us could learn from them. Three things occurred to me.

1. It is important, indeed essential, to find and maintain a life purpose.

2. The key to discovering and maintaining the life purpose is a sense of passion.

3. The underlying component of that purpose and passion is a profound appreciation of the dignity of every person and a commitment to respecting that dignity.

1. It is important, indeed essential, to find and maintain a life purpose. Dr. Jackson discovered the purpose of his life early on: he was to be a doctor and spend his life healing others. Some people find their life purpose in their childhood; for many of us, the life purpose emerges as we go along, and may even change dramatically in the course of our lives. Many young people, leaving college, set their sights on making as much money as they can. They may succeed, but later in life they realize that while the money and all it can buy are fine, there is something missing. In many instances they find that their hearts are moving them in the direction of caring for and helping other people.

Jane was a successful magazine editor and writer when the birth of a son with multiple health problems changed the focus of her life. As she became increasingly involved in caring for him, she began to realize a sacred and precious quality to life, to see life with a depth and richness that had not been there before. As she pursued this new realization, she found herself more and more drawn toward God. This grew into a sense that she was called to serve God and to bring others to him. Today she is an interfaith minister using her religious convictions and her relationship background to help couples to prepare for marriage and to enrich their relationships as husbands and wives.

When one's life purpose is not immediately evident early on, there may be hints as to the course one's life will take. In my own case, I had an uncle who was a priest, and his example and companionship got me thinking about the priesthood. What is especially interesting is that my uncle devoted as much time and attention to his other nieces and nephews, none of whom chose to pursue a religious vocation. His influence touched my spirit in a different way than it touched theirs. What is even more fascinating is that while I was being drawn to the priesthood as a child, I was also being drawn to radio. The radios in our house were a source of profound fascination for me. On my sixth birthday I was given a radio of my own, and before long, as the old song says, "Fascination turned to love." Eventually I was "broadcasting" in my bedroom, using my lamp as a microphone and my record player as a turntable. Who could have guessed that eventually my interest in the priesthood and my interest in radio would create a radio ministry?

Circumstances may refine or even alter one's purpose. Should one become ill, for example, one's focus might shift toward getting well, which might eventually lead to the discovery that one wants to devote oneself to healing others. In *Stages of the Soul*, I wrote of my friend Dr. Catherine Helene Toye, whose sudden debilitating illness closed her medical practice but eventually opened the door to a life of spiritual healing of herself and of others. Dr. Toye was an agnostic at the time she was diagnosed with Ménière's disease; today she is an ardent believer in the power of God.

Is life purpose simply one's career or job? When I speak of a sense of purpose in life, I am speaking in very practical terms. In a sense, one could say that Dr. Toye's life purpose didn't change, that it was a healing purpose all along. That's fine, but I think that approach is a little too esoteric for most of us. I think of life purpose as what we focus on, what we live for—whether that purpose is shallow and narrow or broad and expansive. If we're fortunate, like Dr. Jackson, our job and our purpose go hand in hand. If that's not the case—and I think this is true of most people—we can at least strive to make our job a means to achieving a higher purpose. We may do our job, for example, in order to be able to support our family and to assure that our children will have a quality education. I know many people whose "day job" supports a nighttime career in acting, their real love.

2. The key to discovering and maintaining the life purpose is a sense of passion.   If you feel that you don't have a purpose in life, how can you find one? Or can you? It's important to remember that the choice of your purpose is entirely up to you. No one can dictate it to you, although people may try. That sounds like an absurd statement, because we all know people whose parents dictated their career choices as young men and women: "The children in this family have gone to law school for generations, and you're going to go to law school too, whether you like it or not." Sometimes those choices have been successful, but we know all too many people who have spent years doing something they hated simply because of parental imposition. In some cases, it has broken their spirits, but it need not be allowed to go to that extreme. It all depends on one's ability to discover an underlying passion.

What is a passion? The word comes from a Latin term that means both "to suffer" and "to allow." A passion need not involve suffering—ideally it should involve joy—but the idea is that you *allow* something to touch your heart in such a way that without it, you would *suffer*. I know people whose passion is to play golf. Writing is one of mine, and so is caring for animals. I know a young woman whose passion is working for freedom for slaves in Sudan. My friend and mentor, Liz Dixon, has spent over forty years teaching people how to speak in public, and is currently writing a book on speech and spirituality.

The secret is, the passion is what helps you to discover and maintain your life's purpose. If you hate what you're doing and it seems pointless, you may not be able to up and quit your job. But what you can do instead is ask yourself, "What interests me?" Because that's what a passion is—something that interests you so deeply that you don't want to live without it. It must be a part of your life. You may not be able to spend all of your time doing it, but you need to schedule time for it on a regular basis.

How do you find your passion? First of all, it's important to say that it's OK to have a passion for anything, so long as it is not immoral and does not hurt you or others in some way. Dream big; imagine wildly and broadly. It's a big world, and there's a lot to be impassioned about.

A good way to find a passion is to ask yourself, "What makes me feel like a kid again?" One of the most interesting "As You Think" shows I ever did was when I asked callers to tell me what made them feel like a kid. People called in with answers like listening to old radio shows, riding a Ferris wheel, and walking barefoot on a sandy beach. Now, that in itself may not fuel a life-changing passion, but it does have a definite effect. It gets you heartstorming. Not brainstorming, but heartstorming—feeling and imagining deep down in the heart, where the action really is. Heartstorming frees up your feelings, gets you right down to your deepest memories of your greatest pleasures. My friend Barbara Sher, who uses this method in her career counseling and in her groups, finds that getting in touch with these happy childhood memories gives us a benchmark by which to measure our deepest joys and to begin arranging the future.

It's also important to remember that your passion doesn't have to be the same all the time, and that you can actually have a number of them. The point is to get your heart free so that it can tell you what it knows. Walking the beach and feeling the warm sand beneath your toes might lead you to read Anne Morrow Lindbergh's *Gift from the Sea*, which might, in turn, get you to realize that you've always wanted to write poetry, which down the road might get you imagining what it would be like to be a writer, which might get you to take a course or send a piece in to a magazine. Before long, you're a writer! Passions breed other passions.

3. The underlying component of that purpose and passion is a profound appreciation of the dignity of every person and a commitment to respecting that dignity. It's possible—and good—to hold the dignity of every person as an intellectual principle. But what I'm talking about here is a heart principle. It becomes easier to do as you grow happier within yourself, which is exactly what finding and maintaining your passion does. The more you focus on your passion, the less you become sidetracked by the real or imagined faults and grievances of others. Stuff happens in life, and it's going to continue to happen; and the more anchored you are in what truly matters to you, the happier you are going to be.

That was Dr. Jackson's secret. I am certain he felt frustrated that his son would never follow in his footsteps. Nevertheless, his love for being a doctor and his love of learning fed his love of life and in turn enabled him and his wife to love and enjoy the presence of their son in their life. Finding his passion enabled him to respect everyone else's. That's why he took such an interest in me, and why he spent long hours visiting his patients in the hospital. Finding your passion in one area enables you to find your passion for life and to respect that of others.

∞

What has all this to do with sacred hearts? One very important thing to remember about Dr. Jackson is that he was a daily participant in church services. As I mentioned, he showed up for Mass, not only on Sundays, but every day. Mass at the hospital was early in the morning, around 6:30; and every morning, there was Dr. Jackson. From Mass, he went to his rounds, to visit the patients in the hospital under his care. Mass mattered to him. His banter about my homilies was more than friendly teasing. He came to church looking for inspiration to guide him through his day.

A dedicated physician such as Dr. Jackson reminds me very much of the Sacred Heart of Jesus. The Sacred Heart, as portrayed in Catholic devotion, is a heart that at one and the same time is burning with love and crowned with thorns. Every morning after Mass, Dr. Jackson would walk the corridors of the hospital and see human tragedy firsthand. He would examine, he would touch, he would diagnose, then write prescriptions and promise to come back later. He knew that the lives of his patients were in his hands. He knew that it was up to him to see that they bore their illness—and, if it so happened, their dying—with dignity and comfort. He knew that he was treating not only them, but their families and other loved ones as well. They, too, needed to be reassured and treated with love. Meeting Dr. Jackson, you just knew there was nothing else he would ever be but a doctor, and you knew that he treated his patients with dignity and love. But you also knew that doing so took its toll. I have seen clergy of all faiths whose faces are lined with the burdens and cares of their congregations. Dr. Jackson was like that. He had a great wit and a ready smile, and his eyes twinkled. Nonetheless, the pain of his patients had worn and torn his heart, and you knew it.

The Sacred Heart—and sacred hearts like that of Dr. Jackson—teach us why the word *passion* means "to suffer." As I've said, this is partly because without feeding our God-given passion, we suffer. But the rest of the story is that when we allow our lives to be passionate, we suffer along with those on whose behalf we do what we do. Dr. Jackson felt it, too, as a parent. He glowed with love for his son, yet he suffered at the limitations the little boy so bravely and cheerfully carried.

The New Testament tells the story of the night before Jesus died. Accompanied by some of his disciples, he went to the Garden of Gethsemane to pray. Hoping they would accompany him (instead, they fell asleep), he told them, "My soul is sorrowful to the point of death." There was a price to be paid for the passionate life that Jesus led. You see the same thing in the prophets of the Hebrew Bible who often were stoned for telling people to turn back to God. They, too, paid the price.

Yet it is a lovely price. There is a beauty in paying it. When you meet a man like Dr. Jackson, you know that his was a life of value. People meeting Jesus Christ knew that they had met someone they could never forget, and so it was with those who met the prophets. Sacred hearts are jewels in the crown of life. They tell us how important it is to have passion and purpose in our lives, and that even the price we pay for that sanctifies our hearts and brings a radiant beauty to the rest of the world.

CHAPTER ELEVEN

Hearts That Are Weary

The Search for New Vision

One of the truly remarkable experiences of my life was my two-year stay at the Church of the Holy Innocents in Manhattan's Garment District. For a century and a quarter, this beautiful church on 37th and Broadway has served the people of the fashion industry. A thousand people a day come to the church to pray quietly or to take part in one of the eight daily Masses or to go to confession. In *Stages of the Soul*, I wrote about the church's Return Crucifix, which has brought thousands of people to God.

One of the things I loved about being at that church was the opportunity to meet so many hard-working people. The fashion industry is a difficult business, and its scope seems to change as often as the fashions themselves. It is a grueling, competitive business that demands long hours and high performance. Depending on one's job, it pays extremely well or very poorly. It is virtually impossible to succeed in the fashion industry without working very hard.

There's nothing like being around people who work hard. It's stimulating and invigorating. And hard-working people are often very generous, especially if they know you are working hard yourself. When I left Holy Innocents, I stayed in touch with many of the friends I had made there, and many of them became generous and enthusiastic supporters of "As You Think," my books, and my other endeavors.

In my time at Holy Innocents, I also had the opportunity to meet people who were truly weary. They would come in when the church opened for 7:00 Mass, or at noon. I would see them at the end of the day for devotions or Mass before we closed the church at 6:00. Sometimes I would just watch them pray. At other times they would stop for a short or long chat. Most of them had been getting up early and working late for years, taking buses and trains long distances to get to and from the city. They were weary; you could see it in their eyes and feel it in their souls.

I knew the feeling. In those days, I was juggling a part-time job (which later became full-time) at the Archdiocese of New York with a full schedule of parish duties, plus two radio shows on weekends. It was wonderful work, and I loved all of it. But at the end of the day—and often enough at the beginning of it, too—I was tired.

The process of heartstorming needs to take into account hearts that are weary. Weariness is a part of life. There is absolutely nothing wrong with it unless it begins to sink deep into the soul, as it can. I saw a lot of that at Holy Innocents, which made it wonderful to be there. Why? Because I had the joy of knowing that a kind word, a phrase in a sermon, a prayer at Mass, or a silent prayer offered privately could powerfully touch those souls and bring them to life. In my time in the parish, I made it a point to look out for hearts that were weary and to pray for them. I wasn't sure I could change their lives or better their circumstances, but I knew I could do something to revive them, at least momentarily.

That became a wonderful goal and mission. The nice part about it was that it was so easy to do. It didn't take a lot of work or a great effort. All I really had to do was to sit or kneel in church, look for hearts that were weary, and ask God to bless them. Interestingly, when I did that, I noticed that I would feel better myself.

I wish I had known about that when I was a kid. Watching my mother put in long hours taking care of a house and a family, watching Dad spend long hours at the office every day teaching, writing, and directing an academic program, I knew that my parents were often weary. Being conscientious people, they took their lives and their responsibilities seriously, and as a result they often saw the burdensome side of life. Many nights one or both of them fell asleep while reading or watching television in the living room. Looking back,

I wish I could have understood and appreciated more the weary aspect of my parents' lives. It would have been nice to be able to help them, as I now can help tired people when I see them, though the power of prayer.

∞

What does it mean to be weary? The word itself reminds me of an old garment that has experienced a great deal of wear and tear. To be weary means to have been worn. In *The Velveteen Rabbit*, there is a stuffed animal known as the Skin Horse who is all worn and torn from having been touched and rubbed and hugged and loved by countless children. That's how it is with us as well. The demands of life wear us out. Unfortunately, our weariness does not always, or perhaps often, come from having been patted and loved.

When we think of weariness, our first point of reference is often the physical. Sometimes the pressures of life can make us feel tired right down to our bones. In her remarkable book *Developing Intuition*, Dr. Mona Lisa Schulz presents a highly readable and detailed account of specific ways in which the stresses of life touch our bodies. The thrust of her book is to help us better listen to our bodies, to the symptoms we experience; and to change our lives so as to make those symptoms and their underlying stresses disappear.

Weariness is not just a bodily matter. It can slip into our hearts, minds, and souls as well. The people I saw in church were not only tired in body, but in spirit. In this fast-paced society, that happens all too readily.

How can our hearts become weary? Earlier we noted that the natural rhythm of the heart is to give and receive. Through the arteries, the heart gives blood to the other organs of the body. Through the veins, it receives the blood back and purifies it before sending it out again.

The heart can become weary in two ways: when it gives too much and does not receive enough in return, or when it is somehow blocked in its ability to receive.

A heart that is giving too much and not receiving enough in return will eventually wear out. Giving and not being concerned about receiving is often touted as being deeply spiritual. When I was in a religious novitiate, I remember that we were given a prayer that taught us "to give and not to count the cost." Understood properly, that is fine. The *Bhagavad Gita* says the same thing: act without experiencing the fruits of action.

Understood wrongly, it can become a recipe for exhaustion. If we are going to be open to the fullness of the spiritual destiny that is ours, we must arrange our lives so as to take in the spiritual, intellectual, and emotional energy we need. If we are in a difficult situation at work or in our family and our emotional resources are depleted, it's important to do whatever is necessary to replenish our hearts. Like the people at Holy Innocents, we might need to spend time in church. We might need to play golf or attend a concert or visit a museum. We might need to call a friend or make an appointment for lunch or dinner. It is extremely important that we listen to the guidance of the heart when it says it needs to be filled up.

In marriage, it is vital to listen to one's own emotional needs as well as those of one's spouse. If your spouse is trying to tell you that you're not spending enough time together, listen. With the demands of career and parenting, it is often difficult for couples to find the time they need to be together. That's a cost that needs to be counted. When it's not counted, a marriage can slip away. Our current 50 percent divorce rate should tell us that we're not, as a society, listening to the needs of marriage.

Too much giving and not enough receiving needs to be checked. It can destroy anyone. By the same token, it's important to gauge the kind of giving that you're doing. I know people who are generous givers, but consistently give things that people don't want and fail to give the things that would be of help. That can be wearying as well. In giving, it's important to be sensitive to the needs and desires of the people we are trying to help.

Too much receiving and not enough giving can weary us as well. There are people who will take, take, take without giving a moment's thought to contributing anything to the betterment of someone else. I am blessed with friends who are truly generous in their kindness toward me. One of the questions I keep asking myself is whether I am equally generous toward them. When you're blessed with such generosity, it's easy to slip into the habit of receiving and not think enough about giving back.

Physically and spiritually, the natural flow of the heart is to give *and* receive in equal measure. People with hearts that are weary need to ask themselves whether there might be a problem with the balance of giving and receiving, and what they might do about it.

∞

Isaiah prophesies in the Old Testament book bearing his name, "Say to those who are of a fearful heart, 'Be strong, fear not! Behold, your God will come with vengeance, with the recompense of God. He will come and save you'" (35:4). These words have given solace to countless weary hearts down through the centuries. In just a very few words, they provide a small but powerful program for soulfully restoring our weary hearts.

Be strong. This sounds like a most peculiar thing to say to someone whose heart is weary. When you're exhausted, strong is the last thing you feel that you can be. All you want to do is to make the world go away so that you can rest. If your exhaustion becomes profound enough, you may start thinking that the "eternal rest" of death sounds pretty welcoming.

There would be a problem, I suppose, if the words "be strong" were meant as an invitation to continue unchanged in your weariness. That would make you like Sisyphus, rolling the stone up the hill only to have it roll back down again. No, the words of Scripture are meant to help us to change that, not to perpetuate it.

Why, then, the words "be strong"? Those special words are meant to help us to hold a vision, to provide an insight that is meant to change our present reality. Often when we pray for something, we pray out of the sense that we do not have what we are asking for. As a result, we often feel that our prayers are not being answered. The problem is that we have not changed our vision. We are looking at our world as lacking in something that we want, and that's the vision we continue to hold, even while we are praying for something else. That's not an effective way to pray. What we need to do first is to change the vision, to allow a sense of new possibilities to arise within us, no matter how strong the evidence against those possibilities might appear to be. Prayer is the glue that keeps the vision current and alive.

In religious terms, what I am saying is that we often pray without holding the hope that our prayers can be answered. We send up our prayers to God like a shot in the dark, hoping that he'll be in a good mood today and help us. That's misunderstanding how God works. He doesn't first call us to a new reality and then help us to see it. Rather, he calls us to a new vision and then works with us to manifest it. Why didn't God put his people immediately into the Promised Land? Because he wanted them to have the vision of the Promised Land first so that they would know it when they saw it.

Yes, but wouldn't they have the vision once they were there? Not necessarily, and that's an important thing to realize. One of the great secrets of life is that we often have exactly what we are asking for but can't see it. Recently, a friend was telling me about praying for a new house, looking all over the place and scouring newspaper ads and neighborhoods with no success. Coming home one day, he noticed that the house across the street, which he and his wife had always loved, was for sale. They spoke to the neighbor, made an offer, and the house was theirs!

There are three lessons in this story. One, often the things we pray for are closer than we realize. Two, before my friend could buy the house of his dreams, he had to have the vision that it was available to him. Three, once he had the vision, he had to power the vision. In other words, had he said, "Oh, the neighbor would never sell me the house" or "I can't afford it" or "This is too good to be true," he would have lost the vision and the house.

So when God tells us in the midst of our weariness, "be strong," he's asking us to hold a new vision of ourselves. He's asking us to hold, at least for a moment, the vision that there is the possibility that we could have abundant energy and enthusiasm. Our lives cannot change unless we hold a new vision and empower it. And they can change if we do.

Fear not. Fear is the greatest stumbling block to a new vision. When we hold a new vision of ourselves, it takes us out of our comfort zones, and that gets scary. If I had given in to the fear I felt the first day of broadcasting school, I would not be hosting radio shows today. As we have seen already, we need to discern our fears so that we do not do something immoral or foolish. Assuming that such is not the case, we are afraid because we know that we are leaving our comfort zones, and that worries us. No matter how bad things are, at least we know them. "Better the devil you know than the devil you don't know," my mother and her mother before her used to say. The People of God in the Bible grumbled constantly about their journey to the Promised Land. Who was this "One God" who was leading them? They were comfortable with their old land and their old gods. Why did Moses have to go and lead them away from the land they knew? It's an age-old story.

To them and to us, God says, "Fear not." Whether it means leaving home for the first day of school, leaving the town you grew up in for a job in a place halfway across the country, politely saying no to people who lean too much on you, or learning to say yes to yourself when you need a break or a rest—it's scary making changes. Some people won't understand what in the world you're doing, and you may not even understand it fully yourself. Nonetheless, the admonition is there: "Fear not."

Here is your God. And here is the reason why we can "fear not." When we find ourselves weary, and courageously face our fears about having to change some of our relationships and activities, we are not far from the Kingdom of God. If we give up an extramarital affair or a chronically unreasonable workload in order to have more energy for our marriage and family, we are not far from the Kingdom of God. If we decide to break free of hurts from the past and thus lighten our load, we are not far from the Kingdom of God. If we decide to cut loose of a tyrannical boss who drains every ounce of our spirit, then we are not far from the Kingdom of God.

Here is your God. That statement should tell us how important our liberating decisions are. We may talk ourselves into thinking that our lives have no significance, and there will always be people in our lives who will reinforce the notion of our insignificance. God is not buying any of that. When we're ready to stop complaining, ready to envision ourselves differently, and ready to act on what we see, scary or not, then we are ready for the greatest realization we could possibly have: *God cares.* Which means that our lives have infinite, divine significance. Say it in the traditional way of the Judeo-Christian religions: we are made in the image and likeness of God. When we're weary and feeling beaten down, we can lose the sense of the significance of our lives. "Here is your God" means that when we're ready for a different vision, God will take us into his arms. He's been present all along, really, though our vision has been clouded.

He comes to save You. If we're still clinging a little to our fears, or partially holding on to our old vision of ourselves, the news that God is here may not seem like very good news. Who would want to have been Adam and Eve trying to explain their sin to God? But even then, and certainly now, God cuts through all of that. He tells us that he comes, not to condemn us, but to save us. He wants us to be in the Promised Land, not cowering in a corner someplace else. He comes to save us. Jesus said, "God sent his Son into the world, not to condemn the world, but so that the world might be saved." How many times do we need to be told?

∞

When we are weary, we can turn to God, ask for a new vision, hold our fears in abeyance, and know that God, who comes to save us, is very near.

CHAPTER TWELVE

Reverent Hearts

Hearts That Learn to See Again

When I was a college student in Kansas City, we lived not far from the Benedictine Convent of Perpetual Adoration. There a group of semi-cloistered nuns lived, and all day and night they prayed before the consecrated host, the Body of Christ. We Catholics believe that Jesus Christ is really, not merely symbolically, present in the consecrated host; and these sisters spent their days and nights praying to Jesus and before Jesus. The convent was up on a hill and was a well-known landmark in Kansas City. It was close to Rockhurst, the college (now a university) that I attended, and often I would stop in to pray on my way home or on a school holiday.

There was a special feeling in the chapel of that convent, a warm-hearted and deep peace that pervaded the walls. Years and years of daily prayer by the Sisters and the countless laypeople who stopped by every day had seeped into the architecture, and one could feel grace oozing out from every corner.

That special feeling of reverence in a house of worship touches people to their very core. We feel a connection with someone other than ourselves, someone infinitely higher and more precious. It is as though we had entered a special place, far away from the chaos and cares of the rest of the world. That's what I loved about the Benedictine Chapel. I must admit that I was not a happy camper during my college years. How evident that was on the outside, I don't know; but inside, I was full of sadness and discouragement. I never felt that I was going to make it through college, though my grades for the most part were excellent. I was shy and nervous and tense much of the time. The Benedictine Chapel was a place of refuge for me. It was like stepping into a whole new world, a world of peace and calm. My high school teacher and friend, Sister Raymond, had said to me not long before, "I wish there was a little more calm in your life." Perhaps it was her prayers that led me to that chapel, for there I found a place where worries and cares could be left at the door.

Everything about that chapel exuded reverence. The chapel was pin-drop quiet, except for the occasional clear chiming of a clock that sounded as though the angels themselves were striking the quarter-hour. The Sisters moved slowly and with great dignity as they made their way to the prie-dieux on which they knelt before Our Lord. The chapel was immaculate. Every square inch of the floor shined; not a speck of dust could be found anywhere. The large gold monstrance that held the Body of Christ for all to see was always polished and bore no marks of stain or smudge. The altar linens were starched and fresh. Everything about the chapel told you that this was a special place.

Perhaps you have known a special place like this—a church, a chapel, a synagogue, or a mosque—that truly embodies reverence. If so, you know how different that place is from the rest of the world. It may be that people rush all around you, put pressure on you, and say terrible things to you—but here, you are far apart from all of that, and there is peace. Even if your world is not so terrible, still the wearying demands of interacting with family, friends, acquaintances, and fellow workers are absent from that place where you can find and feel your truest self.

Praying or contemplating there, you may find yourself talking over some of those burdens with the One Who Listens. Taylor Caulfield wrote a series of essays that eventually became books called *The Man Who Listens* and *No One Hears but Him*. In her writings, the special place was a quiet room at the top of an office building where, one by one, in a steady stream, troubled people came to bare their souls. The amazing peace and light that filled the room let them feel accepted, heard, and understood by someone other than themselves, someone infinitely loving and divine. That's how I felt in the

Benedictine Chapel. It's how we all feel in an atmosphere of reverence.

Reverence, of course, is not only found in churches. When I give retreats or days of recollection to married couples, I often remind them of Jesus' words to his disciples, "I am going to prepare a place for you." I tell them that if they want to find their special place, they should look into each other's eyes. When they do that, I see reverence and love. Interestingly, the quality of that reverence varies depending upon how long they are married. Newly married couples have a newness about their reverence that is beautiful to see. Couples married longer have a depth to their reverence that is truly comforting and precious.

Something similar happens with animals. Treat an animal with reverence, and you will be amazed at how his or her eyes reflect a special softness and love when you're around.

Our hearts were made for reverence, to experience and to live in reverence. Why have we forgotten that?

The word reverence has roots that mean "to see again." When we experience reverence, it is as though we are experiencing something that we had forgotten. The peace I experienced in the chapel seemed too good to be true. It seemed as if it should have been an image rather than a reality. When I was back in my ordinary mode, that peace seemed like a mirage. But was it really a mirage? Or was I seeing something that I knew, but had forgotten?

Some five centuries before Christ, Plato taught the youth of Athens his theory of reminiscence. Plato believed that the world we see, our normal base of operations, is just a shadow, an illusion. The real world, he said, contains the unchanging ideas or essences of the things that we interact with every day. Before we were born, he opined, we lived in the world of ideas; but the shock of having our souls joined to our bodies at birth caused us to forget about the real world. From time to time, we get an intimation, a glimpse, of that other world. We can, through study, purify our minds and hearts so that we can remember more of the ideas and even experience them again for ourselves.

Not everyone agrees with Plato—a most notable opponent was his own pupil Aristotle, who believed that the world of our experience was most certainly real. To me, however, there is something about Plato's theory that makes great experiential sense. While I'm not sure I want to go so far as to say that the world we experience every day is an illusion, nonetheless, when we're living at just the level of this world, we do tend to feel that something is missing, that things are not quite right. *What happened?* we ask ourselves. We played by the rules, did everything right—and the bottom fell out on us. Or we played by the rules and had a lot of success, but still felt dissatisfied and discontented. *Life is unfair!* we cry.

Alternately, there are those "peak" or "a-ha" moments when we do get a sense of rightness. That's what I experienced in the Benedictine Chapel. The calm and tranquility of that house of worship was so different from the world of my everyday life, and my heart told me that I was experiencing something that was truer—more authentic—than the world I had left at the door. When my married couples look into each other's eyes to find their special place, sometimes they experience an old feeling that they wonder at having forgotten. "How could we have let this slip away?" they ask each other.

Sometimes these intimations of a more authentic world come under the guise of coincidences. Perhaps someone comes into your life and gives you just the piece of information you have been looking for. I find this often enough when I write. If I'm looking for an example or a story to exemplify a point I am trying to make, often that very thing will play itself out before my eyes. When looking for a story for a sermon, I'm likely to find it in the next book I pick up. It's uncanny.

Occasionally, these things happen in reverse. Someone will show up in my life and give or bring me something I didn't know I wanted, but that I must have been praying for at some level. The love stories in the Bible often manifest this same kind of reverse happenstance quality. Tobias, in the Book of Tobit, going to Media to bring treasure back to his dying father, is led to Sarah and takes her for his wife. Boaz goes to inspect the gleaning of the fields, only to meet Ruth and marry her. We may not know our heart's desire, but there is something that is driving us to find it nonetheless.

Reverence means "seeing again" something that we saw once before and forgot, and now recognize when we see it again. What we see is the very essence of reality, the very truth of being and life. And we honor that in the person or the situation that is presently in our life.

What do we mean by "the very essence of reality, the very truth of being and life?" We can take our lead from Plato, who said that the ideals were eternal, universal, and necessary.

Eternal   When we look at the eternal, we not only see the beauty of someone or something. We are also seeing that quality as everlasting. The beauty I see in someone I love is not something that changes according to sickness or health, riches or poverty, good times or bad times. It is something that perdures, that lasts forever. That is why when people in my life are not acting as they should, I can continue to treat them with reverence. I see beyond their actions to the person inside. That doesn't mean that I condone their actions or support what they are doing. It means that I love them for the human beings they are, even though they are doing things that I do not approve of. I may choose to let them know of my disapproval. I may openly refuse to tolerate any abusive behavior they may be guilty of. Nonetheless, I treat them with reverence. I look beyond their actions to their essence.

This is true also of how I regard myself. There may be times when my behavior is not at its best. Or my behavior might be fine, but my job performance may be down. Perhaps I'm not feeling well or someone has been mean to me, and I am down on myself. In all of these circumstances, I can treat myself with reverence. I, too, am a child of God, the same as everybody else. When I tend to be down on myself, I can remember that and instead see the essence of who I am.

Universal   The philosopher Alfred North Whitehead spoke of "the fallacy of misplaced concreteness." In ordinary language, he was saying that we often confuse what we mean by concreteness. When we say, "Give me a concrete example of what you are talking about," we are implying that universal predications or statements are up in the clouds, but examples are concrete. Concrete means down-to-earth, where we live. "Don't talk to me in generalities," people sometimes tell us. "Be specific, be concrete."

But if down-to-earth, everyday things are so concrete, how come we're so confused about them so often? Much of the time, it's our concrete, everyday lives that are complicated; and what we're longing for is something simple and external to them that will help us to get rid of the complexities. "Give me something simple to do to get out of this mess," people will often say to me. The answers are not found in many of the techniques they have tried, because often those techniques are complex and do nothing to resolve the complexity in which those people are living.

Heartstorming is different, because, while starting with the turmoil and complexity of people's lives, it draws them through heart, mind, and soul to what is simple and concrete. It's what Plato meant when he talked about the universal ideas being the essences of the things that we see. Plato was telling the Athenians that reality was far less complicated than they were making it. At root, reality was simple because it was universal. When you know what the essence of a human being is, or what the essence of a plant is, many of the questions about them resolve themselves. Should I do this or that? The answer lies in knowing whether what you are thinking about doing is consistent with your nature as a human being. When you know the essence of something, it's much easier to try to resolve the apparent complexities in everyday life. It's the same with a lot of things. Open the hood of a broken-down automobile to me, and I'll see a whole bunch of parts whose workings and interrelationships I know nothing about. Put that same car in front of a mechanic, and he'll know exactly what to do. Why? Because he knows the essence of cars—what they are, basically, and how they work. So when he sees *this* car, it's obvious what needs to be done.

Necessary   We spend so much of our lives dealing with contingencies. We make all sorts of plans for the day, only to find them interrupted by phone calls, E-mails, and emergencies. What should have been a simple negotiation for an important business deal turned out to involve countless hours of frustrating meetings. After a while, we can get to thinking that life is nothing but contingencies, and that we lack the ability to plan or count on anything at all.

Is there anything we can really count on to always be true and always be there? The essences of things—the very heart of ourselves as human beings, the nature of love, the meaning of truth—those are the things we can count on, if we take the time and trouble to get to know them. People don't believe that these days, but it's true. People have been so hurt and so ripped off by parents, spouses, traveling salesmen, bosses, friends, and political and religious leaders, that it's hard for them to believe that anything is really true or really reliable. I think that's why Mitch Albom's book *Tuesdays with Morrie* struck a chord in Americans' hearts. As Morrie became progressively infirm, he increasingly focused on what was truly important to know about life and to value in life.

The message is: don't wait. Do the work, ask yourself what truth really is, what decent behavior really demands, what justice really involves—think about these things, ponder them, and you'll begin to see what can be counted on in life. Plus, you'll begin to see that *you* can be counted on. That may be a new idea for you. Maybe the relativism of the age and the meanderings of your own heart have left you wondering whether you can count on yourself, much less be available to others in an effective way. As you begin to see what can really be counted on, you'll find that your heart moves in the direction of those things—it favors them because it knows they will last. Your heart will increasingly want to live in justice, to stand up for the truth, including the truth about who you are. No longer will it settle for accepting the truth of others about you, which often said that you were no good and would never amount to anything. Now it will help you to see your own personal truth in the light of the truth of being. No one will ever again be able to tell you that you are without worth. As Jesus put it, "A sparrow is worth five pennies. You are worth more than *many* sparrows" [emphasis mine]. Tell that to the next person who opines that you are not worth two cents!

That's what we see again when we have reverence. We have forgotten how precious we are, how precious life is. With reverence, we are brought back to universal, eternal, and necessary truths and values. Seeing them, we see ourselves and our lives in a whole new way.

∞

The New Testament (in the eighth chapter of the Gospel of John) has a wonderful story about a woman who was caught in adultery. She was about to be stoned by some religious leaders, who brought her to Jesus because they wanted to trap him, too. They hoped he would tell them to let her go, and thus they would have grounds for punishing him as well.

It was a complicated situation for Jesus. According to her accusers' narrow law—and perhaps misguided rendering of it—this woman had to be stoned. (The law actually called for *both* the man and woman to be stoned. This may explain why Jesus was reluctant to condemn her alone.) The woman was distraught; the tempers of the men were rising. In the midst of all of the chaos and confusion, Jesus calmly bent down and wrote something—we know not what—on the ground. I think that in taking that moment to break from the confusion, Jesus saw that what this was really about was people who had lost sight of the most important thing in life: reverence. In their zeal to condemn the sin, these men had lost sight of both the person who had sinned and the law. They had lost sight of Jesus, whom they also longed to condemn. And they had lost sight of themselves, since apparently they thought themselves to be better than the woman and Jesus. With the eyes of his heart, mind, and soul, Jesus stood up and very respectfully and with great reverence for everyone resolved the complexity by going out of the situation and to a general principle of reverence. "Let him who is without sin," Jesus said, "cast the first stone." Telling the woman to sin no more, he sent her on her way. Her accusers had surreptitiously slunk away in great embarrassment.

In the complexities of our lives, with the half-truths and untruth we allow to guide us, we, too, can take a breath, look to the eternal, universal, and necessary principles of life, and with reverent eyes see again into the truth of things.

CHAPTER THIRTEEN

Heartily Sorry

Helping the Heart Learn

When I was in the first grade, it was somehow deemed that I had reached "the age of reason." In practical terms, that meant that I had developed sufficiently to know the difference between right and wrong. I was a bit puzzled by that, because my parents had been punishing me for doing wrong for years. I remember that spanking I received at age three for misbehaving in church. If I was not able to distinguish between right and wrong, why was I punished?

The marking of my attaining "the age of reason" was not insignificant, however. In the eyes of the Catholic Church, it meant that I was eligible to receive the sacraments of Reconciliation and Holy Eucharist—confession and communion, as we called them back then. Even so, the reception of the sacraments was not automatic. It required a great deal of preparation, including the memorization of numerous questions and answers in the Baltimore Catechism about why God made us and how we were to know, love, and serve him in this world so as to be happy with him in the next. It was a wonderful mental exercise and taught us a storehouse of knowledge about our faith.

Part of preparation for receiving the sacraments was learning to go to confession. In those days, what we called the Sacrament of Penance was administered exclusively in a confessional, a three-roomed booth with the priest in the center room and penitents on either side. A screen separated the priest and the penitents so that the person going to confession could not be seen. Today, face-to-face confession is permitted in a tastefully appointed reconciliation room, but that was not the case in 1953.

In the weeks before our first confession, the Sister taught us to say our Act of Contrition, the prayer we would say after confessing our sins. The prayer—and almost every Catholic can recite this prayer from memory—begins, "O my God, I am heartily sorry for having offended Thee." One of the ways we managed to try the Sister's patience was by our confusion over the words "heartily sorry." For most of us, no one in our lives had ever used the word "heartily," much less "heartily sorry." But at age six, we had all heard the word "hardly." Our unaccustomed ears and tongues managed to turn "heartily sorry" into "hardly sorry": "O my God, I am hardly sorry for having offended Thee" wasn't exactly the sentiment Sister wanted us to have in confession. Her patient drilling at school, reinforced by my parents at home, got me past being "hardly sorry" at last; and on the day of my first confession, in May 1953, I was definitely "heartily sorry" for my sins.

In the years since Vatican II in the 1960s, when the Catholic Church made important changes in some of its teachings and practices, I have heard people publicly and privately ridicule the training we received for the sacraments in Catholic grammar school. I have always hated that ridicule, because I think Catholic education in those days provided an invaluable grasp of the Catholic faith and gave students remarkable pedagogical tools. Kids might not have fully comprehended the meaning of what they were hearing, but they had a solid basis for growing into their faith. For me, words like "heartily sorry"; "Tenebrae," (a service of lights held on Good Friday); and "*totius quotius* indulgence" (graces attached to prayers for the souls in Purgatory on the Feast of All Souls—you received these special graces each time you entered the church) gave my faith an aura of transcendence and made it feel special and mysterious. It made me feel important, too, as though I were part of something sacred and wondrous.

As I've grown up, the phrase "heartily sorry" has become a very significant one for me. As a kid, many times I apologized simply to get myself out of trouble—not so much because I especially cared about offending my mother, but because I was afraid I would be punished for my misdeed. *That* was not being heartily sorry.

As I grew older, I learned that there was a lot of *un*heartly sorrow in people. As a priest, I see it all the time. Companies mistreat some of their best employees and, when they leave, tell them how "sorry" they are to be losing them. More often than not, it means nothing. Businesses give customers delivery dates for goods and services to be rendered, inconvenience those customers by not honoring the dates, and say they're sorry, all the while showing no real interest in resolving the difficulty they have caused. A husband brings home flowers just to avoid a confrontation with his wife about his abusive behavior, and says, "Honey, I'm sorry," and wonders why she isn't impressed. Modern life holds a myriad of ways in which people say they are sorry without it being heartfelt.

∞

What does it mean to be heartily sorry? To be truly from the heart, sorrow must have the following qualities:

1. **Be honest.**

2. **Seriously resolve to do things differently.**

3. **Revere and respect the person offended.**

1. **Be honest.**   Being heartily sorry means that I truly recognize that I either have done something serious to hurt or

offend someone, or have done something that the other person believes to be serious. I'm not heartily sorry if my thoughts, words, or actions have offended another person but I don't care. If I think that the other person is playing victim or that her protestations of being offended are silly or out of line, any apologizing I do will not be heartfelt. To be heartfelt, my apology must come from the bottom of my heart. It must come from the realization that I have done something seriously offensive to someone else.

If you don't agree with the other person's assessment of what you did, but you wish to apologize, being heartily sorry means that your apology must speak to the fact that the other person is offended. In other words, you may be sorry that you have hurt someone, even though you did not intend to hurt that person and do not believe that what you said or did should have hurt him. For example, John thought that Mary was foolish to be hurt by a remark he made in teasing. When she unleashed a considerable amount of anger at him for what he said, he really thought she was blowing things all out of proportion. Yet he was genuinely sorry to see Mary hurting. He gave the matter a great deal of thought, talked it over with some friends, and came to the same conclusion in the end. While he resolved to try to be more sensitive to Mary's feelings in the future, John didn't feel good about apologizing for something that shouldn't have offended her to begin with. Still, he wondered, was there any way to make a sincere apology, one that would be true and still not take more responsibility than was rightly his? John realized that he could apologize for the fact that he had done something to hurt Mary. From the bottom of his heart, he really didn't want to hurt her. His first order of business, then, was to be honest about what he could apologize for, and do that. Perhaps later, he and Mary could talk about why she reacted as she did; but that conversation couldn't take place unless John apologized for his part in the hurt. Without some recognition of her feelings, Mary wouldn't be ready to hear what John is saying.

What if, instead, he tried to apologize for what he did as well as for the hurt he caused? The apology wouldn't be honest or sincere. It might get him through the moment, but it wouldn't be long before he did the same thing again. Someone I know believed that she was treated rudely by her employers and colleagues, and that she was unfairly singled out among her co-workers for responding with annoyance to their treatment of her. The matter was addressed, and the supervisor, without making an actual apology, expressed her concern that the matter be settled and that my friend feel welcome in the company. The next day, that same supervisor again treated my friend rudely. The protestations of a desire for peace apparently did not run very deep, and their sincerity was highly questionable.

To be heartily sorry, your sorrow must be honest and sincere.

2. Seriously resolve to do things differently. In the Roman Catholic tradition, we speak of having a "firm purpose of amendment" when we say we're sorry. In other words, we really intend to do things differently. The people in my friend's office had no firm intention of changing their behavior toward her. They said words that sounded as though she should expect different treatment from them, but there was no substance to their protestations. If someone tells us she is sorry for what she has done, yet turns around and does it all over again, the apology is not sincere. The proof is in the pudding. When I am heartily sorry for what I have done to someone else, I am making a commitment to take whatever steps are necessary for me to stop that behavior. If the behavior is physically or emotionally abusive, for example, it's not enough for me to say, "I'm sorry." I have to be willing to get into therapy, undertake a renewal program, get clean or sober—in other words, take whatever steps are necessary for me to change my behavior. Being heartily sorry requires giving our sorrow legs.

There's a three-letter word that often passes for heart-based sorrow, but does more to undermine it than just about anything else: "try." When I hurt someone and then tell him, "I'm *really* sorry. I'll try to change my behavior," I'm not telling him anything, really. A commitment to try is no commitment at all. It sounds nice. It sounds serious. But it's a weasel term—if I fail, which I obviously think I will, then I have a way of getting myself off the hook. Trying means making less than a real effort and taking less than full responsibility for it. So when I say I am sorry and I'll *really* try not to do it again, you have every reason to feel that I am not heartily sorry.

We often forget that at its root, the heart wants no half-measures. It really wants to commit itself fully. It may entertain a wide variety of feelings all at once, but that is by way of extending an invitation to love what is true and good. When it comes to sorrow, the heart wants you to commit yourself to doing things differently. In the Bible and tradition, this is epitomized by the Greek word *metanoia*, which means "change of mind" or, by extension, "a knowing that goes beyond." When I was teaching college students, I used to tell them that the sort of change suggested by *metanoia* would be similar to someone undergoing a brain transplant. She would see the world differently and have different thoughts and feelings from before. But now, upon further reflection, I see it's not quite as mechanistic as all that. There's an aspect of *metanoia* that means "a knowing that goes beyond." That has a couple of connotations. First, it means that we know something now that goes beyond the limitations of what we knew before. For example, when I am "heartily sorry," it means that I know that my previous patterns of behavior didn't work at building our relationship, and I now know that I need to get beyond them and do something different. But second, it means that my knowing is of an order that is, of its very nature, "beyond": it is not about taking what is already there and fixing it or adapting it, but rather it is about knowing in a whole new, spiritual way.

3. Revere and respect the person offended. That new, spiritual way is the way of respect and reverence. Both words (we have already discussed reverence) come from roots meaning "to see again" or "to see anew." It's not just that we see new things about the other person (and about ourselves): it's that we have a whole new way of seeing him. Let's take an example. In his various books and tapes, Wayne Dyer talks about the difference between his first marriage and his second (present) one. Years ago, Wayne admits, he thought of his wife as being somehow his possession: "my" wife. That led to his developing certain expectations about what she should do and not do, and to strong dissatisfaction if she didn't fulfill those expectations. Today, he says, he cannot conceive of thinking of his wife as a possession. Rather, she is a person in her own right, one who pursues her own spiritual path and who supports him in his. This whole new way of seeing his wife has made his second marriage infinitely richer than his first.

Notice that this is very different from seeing new things about someone. Let's take another example—say there's someone I find it impossible to get along with. I talk to a mutual friend about it, who says to me, "Yes, but he's such a good person. He has so many friends and is so generous to everybody. Try to get along with him." Even though I have new information about that person, it's still going to be difficult to change my feelings about him. I still don't see him in an entirely new way. Suppose, on the other hand, I discuss the problem with another mutual friend who says to me, "Think of him as your teacher. He is teaching you patience and kindness; and when you learn those lessons from him, he'll either go away or you'll have a friend for life." Now, *that* does more than help me to see good qualities in someone I dislike; it helps me to see him in an entirely new way, with new eyes, as it were. That's what *metanoia* means: I have a whole new way of seeing someone. Interestingly, it also gives me a new way of seeing myself. Before, I was a victim of someone else's unpleasantness. Now, I am not a victim, but a student, using this encounter to advance along my path in life.

That's the deepest meaning of being "heartily sorry." In the final analysis, when we choose to be heartily sorry for what we have done to another person, it is because we have come to see that person in an entirely new way. I realize that this individual is in my life for a special reason—to teach something, to bring me to a new place, or to give me love. I realize that I have treated her unfairly (or she thinks I have). Instead of living in guilt or making a superficial and insincere apology, I use the painful result of my former way of acting to move me in the direction of seeing her as a messenger bearing an important truth for me. I see her with new eyes, with reverence and respect for the mission she is on in the world and in my life at this particular time. I realize that I hurt that other person because in some way I didn't recognize what she was bringing into my life. As a matter of fact, I may still not realize it or understand it fully. Nonetheless, I see her now with respect, because I know she has a role to play in my life.

Again, I see myself in a new way as well. Instead of seeing myself with guilt as an adversary of this other person, I now see myself, through being heartily sorry, as a channel for her to experience grace and healing and light.

∞

The biblical story of David and Saul shows us what being heartily sorry can do. Saul has been envious of David and has been looking to kill him. As it's told in 1 Samuel 24, David sees Saul, who has come into a cave to relieve himself. David comes upon him from behind and cuts off an end of Saul's robe. Then, horrified at what he has done, David refuses to allow his men to attack Saul and kill him. Instead, he says, "I will not raise a hand against my lord, for he is the LORD's anointed and a father to me." David continues to see Saul as the anointed of the Lord, and does not allow Saul to become an enemy in his eyes. David keeps his heart and vision pure. David's attitude turns Saul's heart, so that he becomes heartily sorry. "You are in the right rather than I," he tells David. "You have treated me generously, while I have done you harm."

That is the essence of being heartily sorry: to see where we have done harm and repent of it. It is interesting to ponder whether Saul would have apologized had it not been for David's steadfast vision that Saul was an anointed person of the Lord. Interesting—and compelling—for it tells us that we can, by our refusal to see others as enemies, touch their hearts as David touched Saul's. The purity of our hearts' vision can soften the hearts of others and breed contrition and healing.

CHAPTER FOURTEEN

Hearty Stews and Hardy Hearts

When my first book, *Good News for Bad Days*, was published, a very kind reader put a review up on a bookseller's website calling the book "beef stew for the soul." I loved that, because it marked the rich, hearty quality that I wanted the book to have and to create in the hearts of others. I learned that, like myself, the person who wrote that review is from the Midwest, and knows what those chilly Midwestern winters are like. As a kid, I remember blizzards in Kansas City that would routinely shut down schools and make ordinary roadways completely impassable. Our little Boston terrier, Spike, would go out for his run and be up to his tummy in snow!

I would like to pretend that I was of that hardy generation that walked five miles to school and five miles back each day, no matter what the weather. I walked most of the time through grade school, and took the bus in high school—that's the truth of the matter. But whether I went by foot or by school bus, those freezing days and blustery winds whipped right through me. My reader, hailing from Ohio, recalls similar experiences, I am sure. So when he talks about beef stew—even for the soul—I know he is speaking as an expert.

My mother made great stews—huge chunks of beef in brown gravy, with potatoes, onions, and assorted other vegetables thrown in, along with a dash of thyme. You would know the minute you entered the house that one of her beef stews was nigh. The pungent aroma wafted from the stove and blanketed the house with its cozy goodness. You felt warmer already. And when you tasted it—ah, when you tasted that sumptuous stew, you were warmed both inside and out. No frosty Kansas (or Ohio) day was a match for such a stew.

We called my mother's beef stew "hearty," and that is just the right word. A chill Midwestern winter's day froze you through the heart and right down to the bones. In my college days, I remember walking home or standing at the bus stop and feeling cold gusts of wind whip right through me. The expression "cold hands, warm heart" conveys a nice sentiment; but those blustery days sent a chill through even the most thermally protected heart.

The word *hearty* has obvious etymological reference to the heart. When we describe a beef stew as "hearty" we are attributing to it what we take to be the normal condition of the heart. The two words that come immediately to my mind are "warm" and "strong." *Hearty* also means "vigorous," "jovial," and even "filling." Mom's stews, kidney pies, and goulashes certainly made us feel vigorous. For some reason, a cold wintry day always made me sleepy—but Mom's stews took care of that in a minute, filling me with warmth and vitality. I don't know if you'd say they were "jovial," but whatever grace they communicated took care of the blues and the blahs associated with being out in a cold day. Filling, indeed, they were—when you had finished eating, it was like having a warm furnace in your tummy, chasing away the wintry chills.

The reference to "jovial" reminds me that another reference to the word *hearty* has to do with laughter. When I meet people who have heard me on the radio, they comment on my hearty laugh. I enjoy that, because my laugh is very natural to me, and I love being amused by the muses—did you know that the word *amuse* means "with the muses"?—that show up in my life in various disguises. A hearty laugh comes straight from the heart and fills the room and those around us with heart.

A hearty laugh is contagious—it tickles the hearts of all around. When I was a kid back in the 1950s, Spike Jones put out a recording, a spoof, really, of the very tearful song, "I Went to Your Wedding." Patti Page had done the hit recording of the original song, which was a very melancholy rendering of the feelings of a woman attending her lover's wedding. No song could be sadder. In his own inimitable fashion, Spike Jones made a recording of the song, with hilarious lyrics sung by Doodles Weaver, who, to punctuate the satire, laughed so hysterically all through the recording that at times he could not get the words out. It was a great recording, because every time you heard it, you, too, would break out into hysterical laughter until you thought your sides would split. A hearty laugh is catching like that. Laugh, and the world laughs with you, they say.

Besides hearty stews and hearty laughter, there is hearty assent. It is one thing to agree with someone intellectually. It is quite another to give hearty assent to what she is saying. Hearty assent is impassioned, because it comes from the heart.

Right in line with my mother's hearty stews is the expression that describes how I was in their presence—a hearty eater. A person with a hearty appetite eats with gusto. He does not merely pick or clean the plate for the sake of politeness. Rather he devours the food with enthusiasm, nay gusto. His appetite comes from the heart, and he loves to eat. My cat, Flicka, was, at twenty-five, a hearty eater—and a noisy one. Come to think of it, Teddy, at seventeen, can put away a bowl of food with enthusiasm, too. With even greater gusto can he complain if his promised food isn't there. My new kitty, Midnight, in three weeks has grown to about twice the size she was when she joined Teddy and me. She, too, is an appreciative eater.

Another "hearty" expression is "hearty thanks." If someone gives you a special gift or does a special favor that means
a great deal to you, you thank her from the bottom of your
heart. Hearty thanks are heartfelt and expressed with great
zest and a happy outpouring of energy.

Last, but not least, when you meet a loved one or someone dear you have not seen for quite some time, you give
him a "hearty welcome." It's very different from the hello
you might give a delivery person or a stranger.

∞

The various uses of the word *hearty* give us great insight into
the nature of the heart when we stop to think about them. I
love this quotation from Thomas Carlyle: "No man who has
once heartily and wholly laughed can be altogether
irreclaimably bad" (*Sartor Resartus*, 1:4). A hearty laugh can
reveal more about individuals than they realize. It can open
up the very depths of the heart and soul, clean out any block-
ages there, and get the heart pumping again.

That's an important insight, because more and more I
sense that there is very little real laughter in our society.
There are a lot of jokes, but little sense of comedy. Comedy,
in the truest sense, is not the ability to tell funny stories, but
rather the ability to have a sense of humor about life. The
root of the word *comedy* is Middle French, coming from
words meaning "to revel" and "to sing." It is related to our
word *ode*. Our problem with comedy today is that we think

of it in the context of television and not so much as an under-lying virtue. The sitcoms (situation comedies) we see today often ridicule persons or situations in a rather dreary and lack-luster way. They do little to instill in us a *sense* of humor or a *sense* of comedy. What I call "the virtue of comedy" is the power of the soul (that is what a virtue is, by definition) by which we are able to see a funny side of life, even in the midst of seriousness and even tragedy.

How different this is from the repertoires of many of the comedians we see in clubs, in movies, and on television. The tendency in comedy nowadays is to tell jokes, many of which are off-color and even ridicule people and things that are sacred. My several conversations with Steve Allen on "As You Think" gave me heart; for Steve, like other comedians of his generation, consistently and on principle stayed away from so-called humor of this sort. They themselves didn't think it was funny, and they had no desire to engage in it or to put it out into society at large.

Genuine comedy, which stirs up hearty laughter, is meant to evoke something deep inside us. The barrage of jokes we hear from many comedians today is not meant to evoke any-thing from within us, rather to keep us passive and enter-tained. Remember, the meaning of comedy is "to revel" and "to sing." The true purpose of song is not merely to give us something pretty to hear; it is to give us something beau-tiful to sing. A song is successful only when it entices peo-ple to sing it. The odes of old were intended to be sung, not only by a bard, but by a society. Comedy, too, is meant not only to entertain, but to generate laughter and humor. Comedy is successful not merely when it has made somebody feel better. It is successful when it has made somebody be funny.

Carlyle's quote about hearty laughter captures the essence of anything hearty—a hearty stew, a hearty welcome, a hearty greeting, hearty thanks. Something is hearty not only because it puts us into a warm atmosphere, but because it elicits from our hearts that heartiness in themselves and in the world around them.

In his remarkable book *Manifest Your Destiny*, Wayne Dyer reminds us that contrary to our usual way of thinking, our environment is not something separate from us. Rather, we are an integral part of our environment, and our environment is an integral part of us. "Your environment is not something that you must either push or it will push you around," he says. "It is an extension of yourself, just as you are an extension of the environment." This puts a whole different slant on our experience of life. Our experiences are not meant to be passively received and reacted to. They are meant to elicit our hearts. They are meant to elicit creativity from our hearts. They are meant to speak to our hearts and to tease them into contributing back as a result of what they have been given.

That is why un-hearty foods, comedies, greetings, or human experiences of any kind are such a sacrilege. They do not inspire us to be the best that we can be. They do not inspire us toward the manifestation of hearty hearts.

∞

The biblical story of Shadrach, Meshach, and Abednego, the three men put into the fiery furnace by Nebuchadnezzar (in the third chapter of the Book of Daniel), has always struck me as a powerful story of the heart. It is a tale of three men with heart, and it is a story of the heart of God.

The Babylonian king Nebuchadnezzar demanded that Shadrach, Meshach, and Abednego worship his gods, but they refused. When the king threatened to throw them into a fiery furnace, the three replied that they would not know whether their God could save them—but, whether they were rescued or not, they would not serve the king's gods. The king flew into a rage and had the three cast into a fiery furnace. The flames were so hot that people in nearby Chaldea were burned, yet Shadrach, Meshach, and Abednego, unharmed amidst the flames, sang songs of praise to God (vv. 48–51).

Nebuchadnezzar consulted his nobles, and learned that not only were Shadrach, Meshach, and Abednego not hurt, they were also joined by a fourth man, who appeared to be a son of God. Nebuchadnezzar was so impressed with what had happened that he ordered everyone in his kingdom to cease from blaspheming against the God of Shadrach, Meshach, and Abednego.

The faith of Shadrach, Meshach, and Abednego is truly amazing. It's hearty, as we've been learning to use the word. What is so special about their faith is that it's entirely unconditional. It is not based on a belief that God will save them. It is based only in God.

That's amazing, when you stop to think about it. Most of us, going into a frightening situation like Nebuchadnezzar's fiery furnace, would believe in God because we knew he would save us. If not, we would reason, we might just as well believe in the Babylonian gods. Too often, faith is based on expected results. We believe that God will help us win the lottery, and if he doesn't we're mad at him. We believe that good people should have more benefits in this life than bad people, and when the chips don't seem to fall that way we become angry with God. We believe that if we do everything by the book, we should experience divine favor. When we don't appear to, we feel cheated.

The faith of Shadrach, Meshach, and Abednego is different from that. It is not grounded in results, or based on whether God will save them. It is simply faith in God. The faith of Shadrach, Meshach, and Abednego has depth and substance. It is faith that comes from the heart; an unconditional, hearty faith.

Another story of faith, this time in the New Testament, also tells us about faith that comes from the heart. It's a famous story, told by both Matthew and Mark, about Jesus casting a bunch of demons into a herd of swine and thereby sending the swine tumbling down the hill into the river to drown (Matthew 8:30–34; Mark 5:2–17). Gallons of ink have been spilled over the meaning of this story.

Reading it again recently, I saw a whole new dimension to the story that, because of my attention to the pigs, I had never seen before. St. Matthew tells us that the two men whom Jesus healed of the evil spirits were extremely dangerous. He adds that because the men were so violent, people refrained from taking the road near where they lived. Looking at this Gospel story with new eyes, I wondered, "Why did Jesus take that road?" Everybody knew, and therefore he did, that it was extremely dangerous to go there. Everybody else found another way to go. Why didn't he?

It seems to me that Jesus put himself into a position similar to that of the three men in the fiery furnace. When he went down that road, he went without a sense of expectation as to whether he was going to be injured or killed or whether he was going to be safe. He simply knew he had to go, that it was important to go, that there was something God wanted him to do there. He knew that he was going into dangerous territory, but his love for God was unconditional, so he determined to go whether or not God provided for his safety in doing what he had to do.

That's when heart, mind, and soul meet in a hearty faith.

It's tempting to see this incident as similar to Robert Frost's "The Road Not Taken." There, the poet, too, takes a road different from the one most people travel by. But there's a difference. In Frost's poem, both roads are equally safe and equally beautiful. The poet seems not to know exactly why he is choosing one road over the other. In the case of Jesus, one road is safe and the other is treacherous; and Jesus chooses the one that is treacherous, knowing full well what he is doing.

A hearty, soulful faith like that of the three men in the furnace and like that of Jesus is one that is all-engaging regardless of the outcome. It is indicative of a stance toward life that says that results are not important—only faith in God is important.

That might sound strange to us, because when we think of faith in God, we often mean faith in God to do something or to be something. The faith of those men and the faith of Jesus was no more and no less than faith in God to be God. Whatever the outcome, it tells us, we know that God will be God.

Wouldn't it be wonderful if we had faith like that in ourselves? We could acknowledge mistakes, take risks, question our certainties, and even forgive ourselves for our mistakes. All that matters is that you will be you.

If we placed that same faith in others, how different it would be from the way we usually do things? Instead of trying to control others—and without forcing them to agree with us and without forcing ourselves to agree with them— we could allow people the freedom to make their choices and to say that in the end, they will be who they are, and that is all that matters to us. We would stop banishing our children from our houses because they married someone we don't approve of, for example. We would stop hating people because they belong to a different ethnic group or religion.

That's unconditional love. It is hearty, soulful love, as deep and contagious as a hearty beef stew or a hearty welcome. It's how God loves—that's why he sent his son into the fiery furnace, and again down that hazardous road.

Hearty love is the love of God.

CHAPTER FIFTEEN

Dear Hearts

Hearts That Are Precious

My original process of heartstorming began with my thoughts turning to song and movie titles that helped me to identify and describe the many facets of the heart. One song title that leapt to mind was the beautiful "Dear Heart," so classically recorded by Andy Williams. It is a song sung in the absence of a loved one, and the singer finds himself deeply missing his beloved. He wishes she were with him, for the night is cold—at least spiritually, if not physically as well. The singer reflects on how the felt absence of his beloved stretches time in a heartbreaking way: it seems like years, he says, since they were together. Both space and time are affected by her absence. The town is lonesome—all it holds for him is a single room and a table for one.

Yet the song tells us something about this lonesome experience that is truly positive. The memory of the dear heart fuels the lonely man's imagination. Soon he will be home to kiss his beloved, never more to leave her. He is lonely, but somehow the loneliness engenders hope and happy expectations that enable him to get through his lonely night.

We do not know whether the separation of the couple is due to a business trip or a disagreement. It doesn't matter. What matters is the sharing of an experience many of us have had at one time or another. There is even an adage for it: absence makes the heart grow fonder.

The song "Dear Heart" is about lovers, but it could just as easily be about friends. The dear hearts in our lives are the people who bring our hearts to life and keep us interested in living.

June, a woman in her mid-thirties, suffered from multiple illnesses that required frequent hospitalizations. Each time she would leave home in grave condition, come back significantly better, and a few weeks later return to the emergency room gravely ill. Her condition was robbing her of her life, even though her life was constantly being saved by the doctors and nurses.

"I'm angry and frustrated," she told me. "I can't do anything with my life, and every time I start to get my strength back, I get sick again."

I'm not a medical diagnostician, but I have learned over the years that medical conditions frequently are related to spiritual conditions; disease is often about *dis-ease*. So I wondered whether this sick young woman might have some underlying issues to deal with.

I didn't want to unduly tax her already depleted energies, but I needed her to understand that her illness might not be about a bad back or bad genes. Could it be, I wondered, that her repeated illness might be voicing a cry from her heart?

To be honest, it was a new idea for June, as it is for many of us. She had come to think of herself as being unlucky, cursed by fate. "Everybody else in my family has excellent health," she told me. "They have careers. They have great, active lives. I'm the one who was left out. Why me? I don't understand."

I knew how June felt. Twelve years before, I lay in a hospital bed, my whole body out of whack and near death. I, too, thought I had been cursed. I wondered why everybody else I knew was energetic and healthy, while I was bloated and sick. *Was I being punished for something?* I wondered. *I haven't done anything to deserve all of this.* I deeply resented my bad luck.

It was after I was better and out of the hospital that a friend helped me to see that my illness might not have been about a painful destiny. For the first time I began to understand that there were underlying heart issues in my life that had expressed themselves in my illness. The thyroid gland is about power and speaking one's voice in life, and my thyroid had ceased to function. At that time, I felt I had no control over my life, and felt I had very little to say about it. I came to see that this was not a new problem, but a lifelong one. I remembered that as a kid, I was sick a lot—that getting sick was the only way I had to counter being in school, which I was forced to attend and which I hated. My conscious mind had forgotten that, but my heart hadn't. My life wasn't completely out of control, and my saddened heart remembered that there remained one avenue of protest—getting sick and, if need be, checking out.

That's why I understood what June meant when she said she was unlucky, and why I suspected that something else might be going on—her own form of protest.

"June," I probed, "you've told me about your brothers and sisters and how happy their marriages are. I see you have a wedding ring, too. What about your marriage?"

That's when June began to cry. Through long sobbing she told me about her husband of fifteen years, whom she adored. How he was in the Merchant Marine and spent most of the year on duty away from home. How she felt alone without him and time after time begged him to come home. How in her heart she felt lonely and unloved, although her head told her that he loved her and she should be content. After all, she had more to be thankful for than others she knew, and didn't he provide well for her? How she envied her siblings whose spouses came home from work every day and were around for family fun on weekends.

Bingo. In all likelihood there was a close connection between June's broken heart and her broken body. Just as I had done years before, June was making a protest. Her repeated hospitalizations were not a matter of bad lungs but a silent protest, a call for help to a dear heart who was always miles away.

The dear hearts in our lives can occasion our getting sick, but they can also help us to get well and to live happily.

They can come in the form of a special someone. They can come in the form of friends. They can come as co-workers or people with whom we share a special interest. Whoever they are, they are God-given messengers of life and love.

When I was studying in Toronto in the mid-1970s, I was riding the subway and saw an ad for CFRB, a venerable Toronto radio station. The ad was about Wally Crouter, the CFRB personality who owned the morning airwaves for fifty years. Back then, in 1974, Wally had only been broadcasting for twenty-five years or so.

The ad told the story of a couple who had lost a son in Vietnam. The loss of their son left their lives shattered, and they had no clue as to how to cope with their bottomless grief. Like many Torontonians, they were faithful listeners to Wally's program and couldn't imagine beginning the day without his interviews, information, and cheerful voice. His powerful presence on the air brightened each difficult morning.

One day the couple decided to go a step further. Since they couldn't have the presence of their own son, they could "adopt" Wally as a son. Though they still missed their son, having their "adopted" son in their home every morning gave them a new lease on life and helped them to go on living. Wally Crouter became a "dear heart" who helped them find life and light in the midst of incredible darkness.

I loved this story when I read it. It would be almost two decades before I myself would sit before a microphone. In my ten years as a broadcaster I have learned firsthand the power of radio to bond listeners to me and me to listeners. We radio voices become dear hearts to them, as they do to us. When Phil from Howard Beach died, and Rabbi Potasnik and I went to his funeral, I met Short Al, Doris from Rego Park, and Eli from Westchester—all part of my radio family and that of many other hosts on various radio stations in New York City. Dear hearts bring life and love across the radio waves, even though they rarely, if ever, meet in person.

∞

The word *dear* has multiple meanings. Its primary meaning is "beloved." But it also means "costly." I remember my mother, on a shopping spree in a department store, remarking, "Those table linens are very dear." They were expensive and, shrewd shopper that she was, she could think of wiser ways to spend her money.

The two meanings are closely related. If someone or something is dear to us, there is a cost to having them in our lives. They empower us to take a piece of our hearts. There's a price we pay for loving them, and that price is a high one. "Greater love hath no one than this," said Jesus, "to lay down one's life for one's friend" (John 15:13) Whether it's the literal giving of a life or the spending of a lifetime together, it's all the same. The love of dear hearts is a costly love, and we would have it no other way.

The love between dear hearts is a felt, poignant love. It would be difficult to name all its dimensions, but three are especially good to enumerate.

Separateness   The song "Dear Heart," which I discussed earlier, highlights the poignancy of separation from those we love. As I write these lines I am watching a neighbor's family dog wrestle with the fact that his beloved family is away on vacation. There are others to take care of him, but those most important people are missing, and he doesn't really understand. At the moment, my cat, Teddy, is upset because I am on the porch only a few feet away from him. He wants me to be inside where he is.

We understand animals' love because it is so like our love for one another. Husbands and wives long for each other during the work day. Babies cry when parents are away from them, even if only in the next room. June longed so deeply for her sailor husband that she became ill. The love of our dear hearts has a separateness about it that is also a longing. We yearn and pine to be with the one we love.

There is another aspect, different but complementary, to the separateness we feel about our dear hearts. When it is experienced in a balanced way, it preserves both our bond of unity and personal individuality. No matter how deeply we love another person, we cannot become that person—we remain ourselves. We want to unite fully with our beloved, and at the same time we want to be ourselves. In the movie *When Harry Met Sally*, there is a scene with which many of my married friends say they can identify. After making love, Sally says she wants to be held all night long; Harry says he wants to be held for thirty seconds. That's the paradox of love—it wants union but it also wants separateness.

The importance of individuality varies from couple to couple. My parents spent their four decades of married life totally joined to one another. Many of my married friends have a strong preference for maintaining individual schedules, interests, and friends in a way that would have simply baffled my parents. Yet in the mystery of love, Mom and Dad managed to retain strong individual traits and preferences.

This tension between unity and separateness comes out dramatically when a couple has a fight. She wants A, he wants B; both of them want what they want. Yet one secret of good relations is the ability of each partner to be considerate of the wishes of the other, even while feeling deeply the importance of his or her own. I often tell married couples, "Be on each other's side, not on each other's back." When they do that, they are amazed to find that what they really both want is inner peace and love. Once they realize that, they often find a loving way to resolve a problem.

Union   Though it can be tested in ways that are sometimes maddening, there is a union between dear hearts that is powerful and deep. It can transcend miles and decades. It was nearly thirty years ago that I met and began teaching with my friend from Kansas City, Joan Caulfield. In those three decades, we have changed professions and moved to different parts of the country. Joan got married; I became a priest. Each year, we correspond about twice and talk on the phone two or three times. Yet across the changes, the miles, and the years, Joan and I remain dear friends, champions of one another's successes and shoulders for each other's sorrows.

Three years ago, a friend of mine met up with her childhood sweetheart. Since their childhood, each had moved away from their hometown and married others. In time, both of their spouses died. Eventually, the childhood sweethearts met again during one of her trips home to South Carolina, and now they are husband and wife. Their bond formed long ago and somehow took on a life of its own and never died.

Healing   The dear hearts in our lives can occasion great healing for us. When life becomes difficult, they can keep us in touch with the tender, loving side of ourselves while our discouragement over our problems might otherwise lead us to forget. When life becomes tough, these are the people to whom we can turn for love and encouragement. They are often enough beyond the pale of the crises and burdens that we face. Yet for just that reason, they keep us aware that there is more to life than our troubles. Thanks to them, we remember that we have inner resources and strengths we might otherwise forget we had. When we do choose to share our burdens with them, they listen compassionately and enter into the discussion with genuine concern for us. These dear hearts enable us to keep on living the tough times.

Dear hearts can be healers in other ways. As we have seen, we may sometimes disagree with them bitterly and then resolve our differences. The power of the relationship enables us to look beyond our personal point of view and toward our mutual good.

Dear hearts can heal our loneliness, at least in part. My childhood-sweetheart friends never forgot each other, were a little lonely without each other, and were lonely after their respective spouses died. Calling upon their relationship from decades before, they found each other and healed some lonely places in their hearts.

There is something eternal about our dear hearts. They remind us that life is infinitely precious. They invite us to stay in touch with the inner longings that keep us tuned in to what's most worthy of our focus and attention. They are dear, and they make life dear to us.

CHAPTER SIXTEEN

Hearts of Dreamers

Making Wishes Come True

"If a little dreaming is dangerous," wrote Marcel Proust in *Remembrance of Things Past*, "the cure for it is not to dream less but to dream more, to dream all the time." I love his philosophy about dreams. I feel very blessed that so much dreaming was allowed in my home growing up. When my friends and I talk about our childhood homes, we certainly have unique backgrounds and memories of them. But what is fairly common is the very practical character of their families. By and large, they were not encouraged to sit around dreaming. I was fortunate that Mom and Dad were great readers, and when I was very young they read stories to me. I remember Sunday nights in the living room with Mom and Dad reading, and a drama or good music on the radio beside Dad's chair. Those stories and radio programs built imagination. I remember turning on the radio after supper each night to hear the adventures of Sky King and sending away for my secret decoder. When we kids got together, we played soldiers, we played Follow the Leader, we played Cowboys and Indians. I remember one particular friend who would usually begin any game by loudly declaring, "I'm the leader." I often wonder what became of him, and whether he carried his boldness into adult life.

My childhood was full of games and stories, with lots of imagination. That's so important for a kid. The right kinds of stories fuel a child's ability to surpass and transcend limits, to explore new worlds. I'm dismayed today to see boys and girls sitting in front of a television watching the frequently violent and sarcastic fare paraded across the screen.

Even sports don't uplift the imagination these days. When I was a kid, I was never very good at playing sports, but I loved to listen to games on the radio and watch them on television. I remember coming home at lunchtime to watch the Brooklyn Dodgers or the New York Giants or the Yankees in the World Series. In those days, most athletes were heroes, people you could look up to. Baseball, football, and hockey games did not erupt in brutal violence. It was rare to read of our sports idols being arrested for abusive and violent behavior. Don't get me wrong—there are wonderful athletes today. I've met many, and they do their best to inspire kids with the upright quality of their lives. But what we see in the headlines and on the field often gives us a very different impression.

It's not just the professionals, either. I am writing this chapter in the wake of a terrible incident in Massachusetts in which two fathers got into a brutal fight at a kids' baseball game and one father beat the other to death, right in front of the children. That's an unusual incident, but it's merely an extreme case of the kinds of things I hear fairly often from parents whose sons and daughters are involved in sports. Athletics used to be a way of entertaining, of setting goals and achieving them, of learning to play fair and to surpass our limits and expectations of ourselves. What has happened?

I think that what has happened is that we have replaced dreams with information. We have lots and lots of information, but very little understanding of how to deal with it in creative ways. We have become number crunchers, interested in our bottom line. Not long ago, when a former president of the United States openly lied about having an affair with a White House intern, poll after poll showed that the American people didn't mind, because they thought he was running the country well. When results and numbers become our focus, we lose any sense of depth. Life gets lived on the surface, and the surface becomes our sole perspective.

It also becomes our soul perspective. More on that later.

Perhaps I'm painting too bleak a picture. A good friend of mine who is a radio news correspondent for a national network assures me that when he goes out into small town

America, he meets a different kind of folk from those of us who live in the big cities. He loves to go out on assignment to Midwestern towns and cities and talk to children, talk to shoppers downtown, visit dairy farms and county fairs. There, he says, he finds a freshness and simplicity of heart that he fails to find in people in the larger cities. I'm happy to hear that. But I'm skeptical, too, because I know how much the "bottom-line" mentality becomes a kind of Pac-Man, nibbling away at goodness and freshness and leaving us diminished in perspective and in what we expect of ourselves and of life. I worry that those still-bright souls will soon get nibbled up by our growing concern for getting ahead.

I see how the lack of imagination and the ability to dream affects people in their marriages. A favorite song of mine says, "The fundamental loneliness goes whenever two can dream a dream together." One of the most important things in helping a couple prepare for marriage is making sure that they are in touch with a dream. It's important that they make it active, alive, and real, and not just something vague and general. These days, there is so much activity around a wedding that I often find the dream gets lost in the process. The bride and groom are so busy arranging the costumes, the reception, the catering, the invitations, and so on and so on, that they lose sight of what they are doing and why they are doing it. They are so exhausted from attending to all the details of the "perfect" wedding (results again) that they don't have the energy to dream, even if they had a dream to begin with.

I like to get brides and grooms to dream in the months before their marriage, and to be very specific about what they want and expect—and to be excited about it. I do this because I know how important the sense of that dream is going to be to them in the years ahead. If they lose their dream, they may lose their marriage. If they keep it alive, their marriage can sustain the blows that life can deal.

When I say their dream must be alive and specific, I mean that it must be something that can really touch their hearts in a way that they can feel. It's not enough to say, "We want to buy a house and start a family." I want them to see, in their heart's eye, the house they are hoping for. How big is it? How many rooms? How is it decorated? What does the kitchen, the living room, the dining room look like? Is there a patio? Are there lots of windows? If need be, I get them going on one of Alexandra Stoddard's or Victoria Moran's books on soulfulness in the home, to get them to really make their dream alive and exciting. The house is especially important, because from there we can get them to dream about their presence in the house, to see themselves interacting with children and, yes, grandchildren. And we can get them thinking about what place God has in their home as well. Granted, what a married couple is building is really inside of them, but it's expressed on the outside. What they might not be

able to articulate because it's intangible, they often can articulate in its expression in a house.

That excitement can carry them through the infinite
details of a wedding, but it can also make a tremendous difference in their life together after the wedding. When a marriage begins to break down, I often find it is because the
couple has stopped dreaming together. When a couple is
dreaming together, they are on each other's side. When they
stop, that's when they often get on each other's back.

When a debilitated marriage is restored, it is sometimes
because both husband and wife choose to work together on
the marriage. Often enough, though, it happens because *one*
spouse decides to work on the marriage, even though the
other is not doing so. Whether they work alone or together,
the goal is to reestablish the dream. It may take a very different form from their original dream, and that's OK. A
dream is always allowed to change and shift, as long as both
partners have a say in those changes.

Marriage is only one example of the importance of having a dreaming heart. I find it, too, in people's approach to
growing old. A number of friends of mine have decided to
retire while they still have good health and can enjoy life.
What I love about these people—some are couples, some are
single people—is that they have maintained their ability to
dream. Some of them have built new houses; others have
decided to travel. One friend has decided to spend her retire-

ment fostering a program to help women who have had miscarriages, stillbirths, and abortions. Others of them have mastered the Internet. In every case where my friends enjoy their retirement, they have a dream, something that gets them beyond their limitations and into a challenge that they enjoy. They are learning that the dreaming heart is the heart that can live a long and full life.

∞

What is a dream? I have never found a better definition than in the Disney song from *Cinderella*, "A dream is a wish your heart makes"—it's pretty simple, and it's right on target. A dream really comes from the heart and empowers you to action.

I guess there's only one respect in which I might want to differ from Disney's definition of a dream. A dream is a wish, but it is a wish with pull and power and drive. When a wish becomes a dream, it is more than just a hope that something will happen. It is a strong and impassioned wish for change. I know that when I think about the communications thrust of my own life.

People who know me smile when I tell the story of how, as a kid, I took the lampshade off the lamp in my bedroom and used the rest of the lamp as my microphone to broadcast news and music. For about four decades, I wished to be a broadcaster. But I thought it was impossible, and did absolutely nothing about it. I contented myself with listening to programs and mimicking announcers and station promos.

My wish became a dream when I took my first broadcasting class, got a connection with IN TOUCH Networks, and began to see possibilities for my wish to come true. I began to really want it, to take it seriously and work on it. I decided to take the plunge and develop my own show, paying for it myself and calling potential sponsors and donors to support the show. I didn't exactly think of it in this way, but what I was doing was taking my wish and giving it legs. That's what a dream is. As I began to make my dream come true, other things came along—national broadcasts, network commentaries, full-time participation in a high-rated weekly talk show. Broadcasters and their families became my friends. Many of them considered me to be one of them. My dream became real.

Notice what I had to do to have a dream. First, I had to have a wish. And for many years, that's all I had—a wish. I wished I were in radio. But I had to do more than wish. I had to turn the wish into a dream—a wish I owned. To do this, I had to go to work, pay for it, raise the money, get people to help me. I had to own my wish, and to a certain extent allow it to own me. That's when it became a dream.

This is slightly different from what we usually think, isn't it? When parents and teachers, say, chide schoolchildren for daydreaming, their fear is that the young people will cripple themselves and ruin their ability to function in the practical world. "You'll turn into a no-good dreamer, and then what will you do?" they say or strongly imply. For that reason, our society discourages people from being dreamers, and that is a shame. True dreamers are people who can own a wish strongly enough and commit themselves firmly enough to make that wish come true. When Martin Luther King gave his "I Have a Dream" speech, was he merely standing by and wishing that all people could be free? Hardly—he dedicated his entire life to that vision, and lost his life because of it. He did, indeed, have a dream. Watch the movie *Young Edison* and see Spencer Tracy portray the long and heartbreaking hours of seemingly useless research that Edison poured into the invention of the electric light. Only his wife, Mary, believed in him. Edison did more than wish he could harness electrical power—it was a dream that brought him poverty, ridicule, and exhaustion. Until, of course, his dream came true.

When a wish takes legs and becomes a dream, it touches both the heart and the mind. When you become a dreamer, you are changed forever. A dream has several important effects upon the life of the dreamer.

1. **A dream brings you from the present into the future.**

2. **A dream makes you a person of passion.**

3. **The essence of a dream lies in the overcoming of limitations.**

4. A dream often goes against what you ordinarily
   believe.

5. A dream takes over and energizes you.

Let's take a brief look at each of these qualities of a dream.

1. A dream brings you from the present into the future.
That's why a dream is really an act of rebellion. We see the
present, find something lacking there, and decide to do something about it. We ask ourselves whether the future will be
just like the past, and we determine that it will not be. Mother
Teresa, who founded the Missionaries of Charity to care for
the poor of the world, looked at the destitute outcasts of Cal-
cutta and determined that she had to do something to help
them. She knew that she could not go on teaching in a private school. She had to do something, and she did.

2. A dream makes you a person of passion.   What a
dreamer does, he does passionately. That's what makes a
dreamer different from someone who merely wishes. There's
a world of difference between a person who wishes she were
a millionaire and someone for whom it is an active dream.
The former wants it and thinks it would be nice if it
happened. The latter is hungry for it, really visualizes it
happening, and works for it. We usually say that a person has
a dream, but it's equally true to say that the dream has the
person. When someone turns a wish into a dream, the dream

begins to take on a life of its own, providing energy, leads, and apparent coincidences in order to facilitate its purposes.

3. The essence of a dream lies in the overcoming of limitations. What drives a dream, what motivates a dreamer, is that things are not as they should be and that there is a possibility of righting them. I know a Catholic priest who, when assigned to be the pastor of a parish, arrived at his assignment to find that the church had been burned down and that services were being held in a small building on the property. The property even boasted an abandoned stable. Within a few years, he raised the money to build a magnificent church; and at Christmastime he rents live animals for a nativity scene in the stable! Now, there's a positive man!

4. A dream often goes against what you ordinarily believe. I'm sure lots of people told my friend that he'd never build a successful church on that site. People told me that I would not amount to very much. The evangelist Billy Graham, I am told, was so shy that he preached his first sermons out in a field just to get up the courage to speak. Who would have thought that he would go on to become one of the most respected preachers of all time? I read recently that the First Lady of the Stage, the late Helen Hayes, was told that she would never become a great actress because she was only five feet tall. Dreamers are always being told that their dreams not only won't come true, but *can't* come true. They steadfastly refuse to believe it, and redouble their efforts to prove everybody wrong.

5. **A dream takes over and energizes you.**   Is the dreamer dreaming the dream, or is the dream dreaming the dreamer? It's hard to tell. We ordinarily think of the dreamer choosing a dream, but I wonder if we might also say that the dream chooses the dreamer? Sometimes, it just seems as if an idea is out there waiting to be realized, and at just the right moment someone comes along and seizes it. My desire to put on the radio a positive, inspirational call-in show that would give people live exposure to some of the greatest minds in spirituality today—where did that come from? Radio was always my wish, and eventually became my dream; but at some point the concept of "As You Think" overtook me and picked me out to do its work.

Elizabeth, a young actress from St. Louis newly arrived in New York, knocked on the door of Alfred Dixon, the renowned speech teacher, looking for help with her acting voice. Little did she know that when Dixon opened his door to her, she met her destiny. She became his student, his disciple, and eventually his wife and his successor. Eight years after they married, Alfred passed away; and for nearly half a century, Liz Dixon has kept the mission of The Alfred Dixon Speech Systems alive, telling businesspeople, struggling actors, celebrities, radio hosts—even me—that "A new voice is a new you." Her passion is touching lives through speech. It seems that Alfred's dream discovered Liz and brought her there to share it and spread it for the betterment of the world.

∞

I promised that we would talk about the soul, and the effects of dreams upon the soul and the soul upon dreams. I made that promise by way of saying that when we become too results oriented, the surface of life becomes our sole perspective and our soul perspective. There are a couple of things to say here.

Obviously, dreams have something to do with results. If you have a dream, you want to see it bear fruit. As I've been saying, a dream propels you into passionate action, and what you want from your action is results. That's only natural. But what if you let the absence of results kill your dream? What if, during those years when I struggled to raise the money to put "As You Think" on the air, I had given up? There were times when there was no money at all, only promises and hopes. Many times, I wanted to quit. I continued because at some level I knew there had to be something more than the results, more than the number of dollars I had in the foundation. That something more was the dream. The dream stirs the heart. It touches the mind and helps it to see possibilities for overcoming limits. But the soul is the really remarkable and mysterious aspect of all this. Remember, we said earlier that the dream dreams the dreamer. I think that's where the soul comes into a dream. The soul is the weaver of the dream, the one who calls it forth from the heart and the mind, the one who calls us forth to be the bearers of the dream. The soul's function is to weave dreams and to call us to make those dreams come true.

I said in another chapter that the soul is the place where the eternal universals live and flourish, things like justice and truth and beauty and love. Let's look at that a little differently now. It is when justice and truth and beauty and love and all the other virtues and ideals single someone out to bring them to a particular time and place that they become someone's *dreams*. Reading an article on Southeast Asia recently, I remembered my boyhood idol, Dr. Tom Dooley, who worked so heroically to help the people of Cambodia and Laos until his tragic death of cancer. Or what about Maximilian Kolbe, the priest who offered his life so that a fellow prisoner in the concentration camps could go free? What about my friend Martha Ware, a dedicated teacher who gives her students lessons in science and—more important—is there for them when their grandparents or classmates suffer and die and the kids are confused about the tragedies of life? Or my friend Rabbi Joseph Potasnik, who, without remuneration or fanfare, was among the first to be at Kennedy Airport to assist the families of the victims of TWA Flight 800? People like them—people like you—are the embodiment of something universal and eternal, something divine. It is a calling, and people who follow that calling readily say that no amount of fame or lack of it, no amount of money or scarcity of it, would make them do it any other way. Something within their soul calls to them, puts them in touch with a universal good or value, touches their heart and mind with it, and calls them to embody that value in a particular time and place.

But it's not just people like them. It's people like you and like me. Everyone has the potential for a dream. I love the opening and closing scenes of the movie *Pretty Woman*, where a man stops tourists on Hollywood Boulevard and asks them, "What's your dream?" It's a great question. Years before, Rogers and Hammerstein said it in *South Pacific*: "You've got to have a dream. If you don't have a dream, how're ya gonna have a dream come true?"

If you have a soul, you have a dream. Souls house the eternal and draw us to bring it to our heart and finally down to earth. Unlike Prometheus, you do not have to steal fire from the gods—you have been given it to bring to the earth. It's in your soul. No matter what, if you have a soul, and you keep your soul closely in tune with your heart, you will find a dream and a passion.

Can't find your dream? Let's play a game. What's your favorite virtue? Is it love? Is it beauty? Is it moral goodness? Is it honesty? Is it purity? Your favorite virtue, the one you cherish most, the one that gives you goose bumps when you think about it, is probably the one you are being called to bring to earth.

Is that too lofty for you? Well, then, what really grabs you here on earth? Is it seeing an abused or homeless animal, or child, or mother, and wanting to do something? Is it seeing a marriage floundering, or reading statistics about how many marriages are floundering, and wanting to help? Is it watching someone come alive when she realizes that *she loves to write*, and wanting to help her toward that dream? When you see something like that, and want to do something about it—there's your dream.

What's your dream?

CHAPTER SEVENTEEN

Working Hearts

The Labor of Love

"My work is the only ground I've ever had to stand on. I seem to have a whole superstructure with no foundation—but I'm working on the foundation." It's not clear whether those words of Marilyn Monroe were meant to be ironic. Nonetheless, they speak volumes about the way we often regard our work. As for Norma Jean, so for many people, work is the only ground they have to stand on, or ever had. And it is amazing how frequently you hear people say that they hate their jobs. In *Good News for Bad Days*, I wrote about a colleague and friend who committed suicide. One of the things I remember about her is that she absolutely hated her job, an administrative assistant position with a large financial company. Almost as striking and unforgettable as her death itself was a conversation a bunch of us had about it at the radio station where we worked. Someone commented how much our friend had disliked her job. Without missing a beat, someone else piped up, "Hating your job is no reason to kill yourself. *Everybody* hates their job!"

To me, that was such an amazing statement: this person, a very bright and knowledgeable young man who had a great deal of work experience, concluded that across the board, people routinely hated their jobs. After that, I started listening more closely to the ways in which people spoke about their work, how they appeared when they went to work. While I certainly wouldn't make the statement that everybody hates their job, nonetheless an amazing number of people do. Their heart just isn't in their work.

A couple of years later, I was over at another radio station one morning putting together some tape for a show. My engineer was a bright, talkative guy who loved radio as much as I did. We got to reflecting about the nature of morning drive time radio—the shock jocks, the "morning zoo" teams, and those kinds of things. I remember expressing dismay that so many stations seemed to feel obliged to program comedy in the morning, often, in my opinion, without much regard for good taste.

"Oh, I can tell you why they program comedy," my engineer friend piped up. "People go to work hating their jobs and dreading what they're going to face in the day ahead. They need comedy to get them going in the morning."

There it was again.

I began looking for people who loved their jobs. If hating your job is so normal, what goes on with people who love their jobs? Or are there any?

"I haven't worked a day in my life." The statement absolutely startled me. It came from CNN's Larry King, whom I was interviewing for "As You Think."

"What do you mean you haven't worked a day in your life?" I replied in amazement. "I've listened to you on radio and watched you on television for years."

"Father," he told me, "from the first moment I sat in front of a microphone to my latest broadcast of *Larry King Live*, I have absolutely and thoroughly enjoyed what I do. It has never seemed like work to me."

When I thought about his statement, I realized that Larry had put a finger on what might be the major problem with people and work. Without actually saying it, he implied that work, for most of us, tends to be something we hate. If we love it, we don't think of it as work.

Reflecting further, I realized that the idea that work was something people hated went back almost to the dawn of creation. The Bible seems to imply that work was the result of the sin of Adam and Eve. "In the sweat of your brow," God tells Adam and Eve, "you shall eat your bread." Work is thus seen to be a punishment given to our first parents as a consequence of the sin they had committed. There was no work in Paradise, but there certainly was work here on earth.

Another memory led me to understand how deeply that belief penetrates our consciousness. I hate to admit it, but I really always disliked school, especially as a kid. (*Parental advisory*: Parents, if your children are anywhere near this book, you are advised that reading this page may be detrimental to their love of school.) Vacations were time for fun, time when I could do what I wanted. School was torture. I remember lying in bed one summer night before the first day of the academic year, angry that Adam and Eve had sinned and that, as a result, I had to go to school!

When I remembered that, years later, I was astonished. Somehow, at that tender age, I had absorbed the notion that work and school were bad and their opposites good. I certainly wasn't alone in feeling that way. Moreover, I had learned to associate school and work with the notion of divine punishment. God, I was telling myself, would certainly prefer not to send us to school or to work, but he had to because Adam and Eve sinned. In my mind, it was similar to times my parents told me that they wished they didn't have to punish me for some misdeed, but that I had done something wrong and they had no choice. So when my mother, exasperated with my resistance to going to school, told me, "If you don't go to school, you'll grow up to be ignorant. Do you want to be ignorant?" I cheerfully replied, "Fine with me." No wonder mothers get gray.

Whether or not we base our feelings about work on biblical roots, the fact is, many of us feel, deep in our hearts, that work is something bad or undesirable and that leisure is something good. Yet paradoxically, we feel a kind of nervous obligation to keep busy, even during leisure time. "The idle mind is the devil's playground," after all. We fill our "free" time with so many activities that we often come away from it more tired that we were when we entered into it.

Another reason that work gets such a bad rap among us is that we have tied it so intimately to our financial conditions. Work is the means by which we earn our livelihood. More and more, couples are holding down two jobs in order to make ends meet in their households. Individuals often have more than one job in order to pay bills and keep their heads above water.

Another negative feature about work for many people is the commute. In a large city like New York, a commute of under an hour is unusual, and it often involves changing buses and trains, or being stuck in rush hour traffic jams. Often it's unpleasant to get to and from work, which hardly makes the work itself agreeable.

As a result, we dream of the day when we can retire and quit work. We fantasize about winning the lottery so that we'll never have to work again. Work becomes a negative for so many. And yet we have to do it.

When we do get to work, it's sometimes unpleasant to be there. We spend eight hours a day minimum with our bosses, and if they're cranky and hard to deal with we carry that with us both to and from the office as well. We talk about leaving work at the office, but it's hard not to bring the frustration home. So many people have to bring work home as well. Huge briefcases of paperwork and the ever-present laptop computers are increasingly the order of the day. Often enough your boss says that you *can* take it with you when it comes to your work—and you'd better, if you want to be competitive and keep your job.

Then there's the issue of co-workers. If you're lucky, you work with people who are nice, honest, cooperative, and fun to be with. If this is not your situation, it's like being married to the spouse from hell. I wish I had a dollar for every horror story I've heard people tell about the people they work with. (And I'm only hearing *their* side!) No wonder they hate to go to work.

∞

What would be involved in loving our work? Is there some way we can change things so that work becomes a happier part of us? Can it be more heartfelt and more loving? Here are some thoughts that can help us to make it different.

1. **Don't quit your day job.**

2. **It's possible to do what you love.**

3. **You can detach your work from your finances.**

4. **See work as a way of cocreating with God, not as a punishment from God.**

5. Reevaluate the role of work in your life.

Let's see what each of these thoughts might do to improve the bleak picture our hearts often provide us about our work.

1. **Don't quit your day job.**   I learned this in broadcasting school, and I'm glad they were wise enough to teach it—because they knew some people would eventually quit. I was amazed to see something on-line recently telling people how to go about leaving a job to pursue a dream. I gather a number of people have just up and quit without a great deal of thought and planning. I'm not saying one should never do that. But there are a number of things to ponder before leaving a job you hate.

In the first place, you need time to consider why you hate the job. That might seem like a foolish thing to say, but the more precisely you figure out what it is you dislike, the better equipped you'll be to avoid making the same mistake in a new situation.

Second, you need to take time to figure out just what you want. Leaving doesn't give you what you want unless you leave *for* something else. In considering this, don't automatically assume that you will leave for another job. Do you *want* another job, or do you want to be your own boss? Knowing that before you leave makes it more likely that your next move will be in the direction of what you *really* want, not what you unthinkingly assume you want.

Third, you need to figure out whether you really want to leave, or whether deep in your heart you want to stay and try to make things work out. A friend of mine who disliked her place of work went looking, but as she looked she also tried to see whether she could make the present situation work. When she did decide to leave, she left with a clear conscience and a better sense that she was doing the right thing.

Here's an unusual twist for you, but it's worth considering. Another friend of mine simply didn't like the conditions where she worked. She felt that the boss was heavy-handed and nosy and that some of her co-workers were petty and unpleasant. "When I prayed about leaving," she told me, "I felt a clear message that God wanted me to stay there and make the situation more loving." That's unusual, I think, but it's something to consider before leaping out of a rough situation.

2. It's possible to do what you love. That thought simply never occurs to many of us. We assume that we're going to have to spend our entire work lives doing things that we hate, or at least not doing things that we love. You do what you love in your free time, but work is work, right? Don't tell yourself that lie another second longer. If there's something that you love, you can build a career around it, whether it's race car driving or fishing or decorating or gardening or landscaping. The way to do it is to volunteer for a while, to get a feel for what's involved. Again, don't just up and quit your

job, but find a way to join a garden club, talk to a horticul-
turist, or volunteer with a stock car racing association. As you
meet people who love what you love, you'll begin to discover
how to make your living doing what you love, whether it's by
working for somebody else or starting your own business.
Don't rule out that possibility by any means, no matter what
anybody has ever told you.

3. You can detach your work from your finances. Most
of us readily fall for the assumption that our work has to be
the source of our income. Yet people challenge that every
day—free up their work from that burden, and do the work
they love. Are they in the poorhouse? By no means. Are they
people who have inherited huge sums of money and never
have to work again? Not the ones I know. Did they win the
lottery? Not that I know of. How do they do it? It varies.
Some of them do very well on the stock market and have
accumulated enough money to do as much or as little work
as they like without depending on work for income. Others
have cashed in on outstanding Internet opportunities that
have helped them to grow financially while helping others to
do the same and to realize their other dreams as well. Almost
all have received some good advice about their money from
financial planners they know and trust. There are many ways.
What is common to all of them is that their accumulation and
use of money is independent of the work they do. They are
free to pursue work that they love without worrying about

whether it will make them financially successful because they have learned how to acquire wealth in other, legal and legitimate, ways. There is no need to be enslaved by a job in which you are unhappy, just because it gives you financial security. You need not tie your financial security to your job.

4. See work as a way of cocreating with God, not as a punishment from God.   Some people think that if the Bible says that work is a punishment from God, they are stuck with that attitude. While the "sweat of your brow" passage is the one most frequently quoted and referred to when talking about work, there's another passage in Genesis that shows us something different. In the second creation story, the author says that "the LORD God took the man and put him in the Garden of Eden to work it and take care of it" (2:15). Note that this is *before the Fall* and has nothing to do with sin. God gave Adam work because he wanted Adam to help him care for the garden. Work was meant to be not a punishment, but a way of God and people working together.

What does the "sweat of your brow" mean, then? It means that, separated from God because of their sin, Adam and Eve will find labor more difficult than they did before the Fall. It does not mean that work is a punishment. We would do ourselves a great service if we divested the notion of punishment from our concepts and beliefs about work and instead saw ourselves as working together with God to tend and care for the earth. We might then choose different kinds of work for ourselves and do our work with a greater sense of mission and purpose.

5. Reevaluate the role of work in your life. Back in the Monastic Age in medieval times, St. Benedict and his followers had a notion of work that we would do well to consider. They said *laborare est orare*—to work is to pray. The monks worked very hard and taught others to do the same. But instead of burning themselves out by working all the time, they paced their lives and put their work into the context of a life of prayer. The monks spent a great deal of their lives in prayer. What we know today as the Divine Office, the prayerful recitation or chanting of the Psalms throughout the day and night, helped the monks to center their days in God and enabled them to take time from their labors. When they went back to work, their hearts and minds and souls were steeped in prayer. When they worked, they saw their work as another part of their day of prayer.

What if you and I could do the same thing? What if we could pace ourselves and give ourselves times of quiet and prayerful rest in the course of our day instead of burning ourselves out in feverish work and activity? It's not impossible. People have been doing it for centuries.

People are doing it today. You might be surprised to know how many of your busy colleagues—people who might not seem religious to you—begin and end their days in prayer. I know a devout Jew who makes it possible for the Muslim employees in his deli to make their required daily periods of prayer while at work. Is work the only thing that's important in life? A lot of your friends and neighbors are thinking differently. How about you?

It's the same with family and friends. How often do we end up telling ourselves and our loved ones that we really wish we had time to get together, but we're just so "busy." One day I came to work to learn that one of my bosses, a quiet, lovely man, had died of a heart attack the day before. It was a startling discovery. I had just seen him, talked to him, ridden the elevator with him, benefited from his kindness and encouragement. It was a valuable lesson to me to take time to visit and appreciate the people in my life. If I let myself get so busy that I don't have time for them, something is very wrong.

It is possible for us to rethink our view of work. Not just work in general, but our particular manifestation of work— why we do it, how we're going to do it, what kind of relative importance we're going to give it. Granted, our society's view of work is pretty heavily ingrained. Nonetheless, we can rethink it, and take responsibility for how we do it and for what we do.

∞

When we put our hearts into our work, we may change our minds about it. What about our souls? To people who are consciously people of the soul, there is really only one kind of work—fulfilling the destiny for which God has put them on earth. Whatever form their labor takes depends on how and whether it helps them to fulfill their mission. I know people whose passion is prison ministry—visiting prisoners, singing with them, and helping them to find God's love in their lives. It's not their full-time job. Rather, it's something they do on weekends and in the evenings. But to hear them talk, it's their true work on earth. Their jobs are fine and they do them well, but it's the prison work that really touches their souls—it's the reason they believe God has put them here. The doctor who introduced me to the writings of Sir William Osler and who showed me the depths of his heart and soul was a man who believed that God put him on earth to heal, and everything in his work, in his relationships with his family, in his prayer, and in his intellectual life was centered in his life as a healer.

People who are deliberately soulful have a way of centering themselves in God, and their sense of work is as broad and expansive as their souls. There is a balance to their work because, whatever their job or occupation, their true work is to communicate the love of God. Their career or profession is a part of that and is fueled by that, but it is only a part. Their work is not the be-all and end-all of their lives, though it is important and they take it seriously. Their true work is to take care of the garden of God—and, like good gardeners, they know how to work hard and work smart and to enjoy the beauty of the work they do.

CHAPTER EIGHTEEN

Heart Space

Finding the Desert Places

"They cannot scare me with their empty spaces / Between stars—on stars where no human race is. / I have it in me so much nearer home / To scare myself with my own desert places." Robert Frost was right about our "Desert Places"— they are often the scariest parts of ourselves. We don't like the spaces in our hearts—we try to cover them up, forget about them, put them out of our awareness. But they are the most wonderful parts of our heart space.

Just the very mention of the term *heart space* is intriguing. A space, we know, is a place for something. Just as surely as we have a space for our bodies, a space for our minds, and a space for our souls, God has designed for us a heart space, a place to put our feelings and our attitudes. "A place for everything and everything in its place," we say, and indeed God has constructed the heart so that our passions, our fears, and our deepest loves will have a space.

Hinduism is much more definite than many other religions about defining the heart space. Hindus call it a *chakra*. The chakras are seven energy centers in the body, and, yes, there is one for the heart. It is in the heart space that a person faces the feeling and emotional issues of his life, identifies them, and brings them into love and light. The heart space is the center of compassion, the place where we recognize and understand the experiences that are part of the lives of others. It is the center of genuine understanding. Most of us can, when hurt by another, achieve a mental "understanding" of why someone would do such a thing. Compassion in the heart chakra is very different. It is *felt* understanding and release.

The difference between the two kinds of compassion is like the difference between the two kinds of charity. For some people, charity means giving money to someone or to an organization that helps people in need. That indeed is one level of charity. But how different it is from the virtue of charity, which enables us to personally love and care about people in need? It's the same with service. There are people who do community service because they are required to do so for one reason or another. They'll do their required number of hours in the soup kitchen, say, and then they're gone. Contrast them with the people whose true compassion for those in need brings them to the serving line day after day, week after week, come rain or come shine.

The heart space demands that we go to that deeper level. It is the place where we live at the level of caring. When our energies are in the heart space, we are not doing things simply out of duty or obligation, not dealing with people from a distance. Rather, we are personally involved. That is what the heart space is all about.

Living in the heart space means letting ourselves be overtaken by the mystery of things. Giving money to programs may be an example of genuine, involved caring, but more often than not it is a way of dealing with things by not having to deal with them. It is giving without having to get involved. That's one reason that very wealthy people sometimes like to dress down a little and head for a bread line or a volunteer clinic or join a literacy program and help others without anybody knowing who they are.

One of my favorite stories about just that sort of heart space living concerns His Eminence, John Cardinal O'Connor, the late Archbishop of New York. For years, he would quietly visit a clinic for patients with AIDS, where he would minister to them physically and spiritually. He dressed simply, with no press around and none of the accoutrements of his position, and quietly made himself present to the suffering and dying patients.

My friend Sister Pascal Conforti has worked in that same clinic for many years, in St. Clare's Hospital in the Hell's

Kitchen section of New York City. "I would be there in the daytime," she told me, "and the Cardinal would usually come at night, and I wouldn't see him. But in the mornings when I would see the patients for the first time that day, inevitably one or more of them would tell me, with eyes bright with happiness, 'Oh, Sister, Father John was here last night.'"

"When this first happened," Sister Pascal recalled, "I was puzzled. I would say to them, 'We don't have a Father John at this hospital.' Then they would pull out a card with a picture of the Cardinal and say to me, 'There is Father John.' The Cardinal, in visiting the patients, had taken on the name and demeanor of a simple priest: instead of using his title of Cardinal, he chose the simple name of Father, the title of an ordinary priest. His simple, kind manner touched them so very deeply."

That's the heart chakra. It needs only itself to make a lasting impression.

Cardinal O'Connor became a model to me of that incredible and intense caring. He was every inch the Cardinal Archbishop of New York, and one of the finest minds I have ever had the privilege to know. He also had one of the most caring hearts you could imagine. About ten years ago, as I was coming to know him, I had the privilege of accompanying him as he visited the various Catholic churches of the Lower East Side of Manhattan. At one point in the day, we escorted the Cardinal to a women's shelter on Madison Street near St. James Church. As he walked along the streets of the Lower

East Side, I was amazed and touched at how readily people came up to him, to talk, to ask for a prayer or a blessing. Some of them clearly didn't know exactly who he was, but they knew his face from the newspapers or television. It happened to be a day when I knew the Cardinal was not feeling particularly well, and this visit was an effort for him. Nonetheless, he had time for every person who approached him. He chatted with them, blessed them, and promised to pray for them. People on the Lower East Side don't approach you like that unless they sense you have a loving, caring heart. They sensed the Cardinal's heart, and they were right.

It is important that we define and recognize our heart space, and make the most of it. To do that, we have to recognize something else—the importance of the spaces within the heart space. If that sounds confusing, bear with me a moment.

Have you ever stopped to think what life would be without spaces? This morning, I rode on a crowded elevator to get to the nineteenth floor of the building where I work. We were piled in pretty much on top of one another, with very little space between us. It was hot and crowded and uncomfortable. We craved more space, more "breathing room," as we say. We need physical space.

I remember seeing a Garfield cartoon in which the opinionated cat loudly proclaimed, "I need my space!" So do I. So do we all. It's not just a physical thing, like the elevator. We also need our space inside. When I lived in the Jesuit novitiate many years ago, we were assigned not rooms, but cubicles, tiny quarters whose walls only went part of the way to the ceiling. If the guy down the hall sneezed or, God forbid, fell asleep during a meditation, you heard him clearly. It felt like we were living on top of one another. Having had my own room most of my life, it was pretty hard to get used to. Most of us need space, outside ourselves and inside ourselves.

Lack of inner space can make us feel like we're going crazy. When we talk about being confused (the word means "joined together"), we feel that our thoughts and feelings are all piled on top of each other, with no space between them. When our calendars are overloaded and we're exhausted from trying to meet everybody's needs and demands, we feel that there is no space in our lives for ourselves. "All I want to do is to carve out a little time for myself," an exhausted father once told me. Inside, he was telling me, he felt like a huge block of wood or stone, and he desperately wanted to create some space.

It's not enough to have a heart space. We must also have space within our hearts. Without space, we simply can't communicate. Without the space bar on my computer, allthewordswouldjustruntogether. We need spaces between them to make them work. It's the same in music. Without rests, the notes would run all together without rhythm. That's what happens with cacophony. A symphony is a symphony because of the spaces between the notes, the spacing that allows for change of movements. Cacophony happens when there are no spaces, and everything runs all together.

Our heart space needs spaces in between the feelings and impressions that run through it. When we're all mixed up and our hearts are racing, it's a sign that we need to insert some pauses.

As Robert Frost said, though, that can be scary. In a way, we're talking about two different things. He was talking about the desert places that we sometimes find within us, and we're talking about inserting some pauses into our overtaxed heart space. Yet we're really not talking apples and oranges, are we? The desert places in our hearts, as we have seen so often in this book, are ways in which God, nature, our unconscious, or some other force beyond us tries to get us to pause and take a break in the action of our lives. When we're feeling down or lonely or depressed or bored or stuck—the desert places—we know that those are signals for us to slow down and ask some questions. Often when we feel depleted, our exhaustion is a sign to us to figure out why. It's an invitation to take a much-needed pause. So Frost and I are talking about the same thing, after all.

∞

How do we insert pauses into our harried heart space when we need to? There is not a special number of ways, but let's talk about a few just to get us started . . . or stopped.

1. "Give me a break!"

2. Give yourself breathing room.

3. What's on your mind?

4. Meditate.

1. "Give me a break!"   I like to help people discover the
symptoms that can guide them into the future. Quite often
these days, I hear busy, harried people exclaim, "Give me a
break!" when someone hassles them or says or does something they consider foolish. Whenever I hear that (or whenever I say it), I can safely say I'm in the presence of someone
who needs to pause. Perhaps for a short while, perhaps for a
good long while. We utter phrases like this so glibly that we
don't generally realize that we're saying something that comes
from the depths of our being. We also don't realize that we're
giving ourselves some very good advice.

When your thoughts and feelings are racing, when you're
"at sixes and sevens," as we sometimes say, it may be a good
idea to give yourself a break. It is seldom a good idea to act
on impulse. If your boss is stupid or mean and steps over the
line in asking you to take on one more project that will keep
you working well into the night for the next several weeks,
your impulse may be to quit. That may be a good decision,
but before you make it, give yourself a break. If you're married with four small children and you're exhausted running

back and forth between family demands and work demands, you may well have fantasies of leaving. Before you do, give yourself a break.

A break may be a minute, a day, a weekend, a couple of weeks—it's up to you. But take one. The frustration you're feeling needs a little heartstorming—it needs to be felt and brought to the mind and the soul, just as we've been doing here in these chapters. You need to stop the flow of feelings and thoughts and get down to what you really want and need. You need some time to line up options and see what's really best for you.

The point of a break is to give some time to let what some spiritual writers today call "The Observer" to kick in. When you're overloaded, you're the victim, or at least that's how you feel. When The Observer arrives, you are able to look at the flow of what's going on and see it as though it were happening outside of you. You watch it with interest, even with objectivity, and that gets you ready to evaluate and to act.

You watch it with *interest*. That's key. When you're involved in a painful or exasperating situation, it doesn't appear interesting, just hurtful or maddening. When it becomes interesting, you are in a position to ask yourself what this situation is meant to teach you, and how it can guide you toward your future. *How did I get myself into this? What can I learn from it, and how can I get myself out of it? Or can I stay, and do it better?*

If that sounds contrived, consider this. Whatever situation you're in, you're in it because in some way it's interesting for you to be in it—that is, there's something for you to learn there. When it stops being interesting, you'll move on to something else or do things differently. I know someone who left a job with a really tyrannical boss to go to another job where he was assured nothing like that would happen. A year later, he realized he had moved into the exact same situation after all. His new boss was even worse than his old one. When we talked about it, I told him, "You must have some interest in learning skills for dealing with tyrants." He chortled when I said that and replied, "You know, I hate to admit it. But I've been realizing that I have some of the same characteristics as those bosses of mine. I've been wondering whether I'm supposed to learn how not to be so much like them." He took time to ponder that, and while he was doing that an opportunity arose for him to work in the same field with someone who was kinder and who appreciated his gifts and talents. He needed to give himself a break to reflect on why he was interested in tyrants, and once he did that, he was free for new opportunities.

2. **Give yourself breathing room.**   One year when we were on a family vacation at a resort, a woman was accidentally knocked down by a kid who was not watching where he was running. She had the wind knocked out of her, and people ran and encircled her, wanting to help. Finally, a counselor

from the resort arrived and told everyone, "Get back! Give her air!" He then proceeded to help her get her wind and get back on her feet.

When in a personal crisis, you would do well to heed that resort counselor's advice. You need to get air, to give yourself breathing room. A friend of mine was fired after fourteen years with her company, when a new boss came in whose style was different from hers. She was given two weeks' notice, and for the first time in her adult life she found herself out of work. "I cried myself to sleep the night they fired me," she told me later. "I didn't know what I was going to do."

"What *are* you going to do?" I asked her. "Do you have any leads or offers?"

"Oh, no," she told me. "I've decided to take the summer off. I'll look for a job in the fall."

I saw her on the street about a month later, and could not get over how good she looked, how stress-free and happy. "I've been to Europe," she excitedly told me, "and I am planning other trips in the weeks ahead." In the midst of her stress, she was smart enough to give herself some breathing room before launching into another job. Whatever career she chooses, she has put herself in the position of not having to take just anything that comes along, and she will have a better sense of what she truly wants.

I can hear what you're thinking. You've lost your job or your spouse, or your computer lost your doctoral dissertation. As much as you would love to, you can't afford to take two or three months off to recoup. Here's the good news: you don't need to. When I talk about giving yourself breathing room, I mean that literally. Physically, mentally, emotionally, and spiritually, you need air.

Lie on your back in a comfortable position, or sit on your favorite couch or recliner. Make sure the radio and television are off, and that the phone is turned off so that you won't be interrupted for a few minutes. Close your eyes, and begin a pattern of slowly inhaling and exhaling. Breathe deep: give yourself plenty of breathing room. As you inhale, see yourself breathing in fresh air. As you exhale, see yourself getting rid of all of the stale air (toxic feelings and thoughts) inside you. Do that for a couple of minutes, until you feel centered and relaxed. It's not a trip to Europe, but it's the way a lot of spiritual masters get deep inside themselves when they need a break or before beginning a meditation.

If you do this exercise from time to time, and if you do it when you find yourself stressed, you'll be amazed at how you'll stay relaxed in the midst of stress and how much more adept you'll be at handling stress.

3. What's on your mind?   One of the interesting things that happens during the breathing exercise we just discussed is that you become clearer about what's going on in your heart and mind. That's because your breathing has stopped the endless flow of feelings and thoughts and put you beyond them.

This gives you the opportunity to observe what's going on. At this point, it's a good idea to identify one underlying thing that's going on within you. When you're in crisis, you may have so many feelings that unless you slow down your thoughts and get beyond them, you'll scarcely be able to identify what's happening.

When I speak of "getting beyond" them, I don't mean what people mean when they tell you to get on with your life. You're not ready for that just yet. Instead, I'm talking about being able to step out of the rush of your feelings and thoughts and get to an inner place of quiet where you can observe them. I work on the nineteenth floor of an office building. On a sunny day, I can watch the billowy white clouds float across the sky. That's what you want to be able to do with your feelings and thoughts. Just watch them go by. Then you will be able to see what issues they are pointing to.

4. Meditate. The breathing exercise is a kind of meditation, but there are others. Meditation is any exercise that puts you into an awareness of the presence of God. Some people meditate by reflecting on a passage of Scripture. Others read a Scripture passage and put themselves into the place of one of the characters. (They might identify with the Bible's prodigal son, for instance, who squanders his inheritance and returns home repentant, but ends up basking in his father's generous love.) Sometimes people take a mantra (like the sacred word "om") or the name of Jesus and repeat it in tandem with their breathing. There is an infinite variety of ways in which to meditate. At the end of this book, I will suggest some resources that might prove helpful. The point of it is to get free from the constraints of the stresses you are under and to experience yourself as free in God. With that realization, you can find yourself asking for and getting guidance as to what to do with that new sense of freedom.

Whichever of these things you do—or whatever methods of your own you develop—it is important that you put yourself into the heart space and allow spaces and gaps in your thoughts and feelings to lead you deep within, to the place where you are truly free.

∽

Can we really ever know God, or is he too far above us?

That's a question we often ask when we reach a crisis point in our lives. A crisis involves the realization that everything we have known no longer works to help us in life. If we are to get beyond the present situation, we must somehow go beyond the knowledge that we have and embrace what we do not know. Either that, or we simply give up.

That sounds absurd, doesn't it? How do we embrace what we do not know? It also sounds impossible—are we to spend the rest of our lives studying and looking for more and more answers to our dilemma? Is that what this means?

We might do that, but there's another possibility. It's possible that the problem lies not in what we know, but in the way in which we know. In other words, our crisis arose because our current answers didn't work. Is it possible that if we developed a different way of knowing, we might be able to resolve our crisis?

Let's take an example. Say I get a call from a couple who have asked me to witness their wedding in a few months. To my surprise—and to theirs—they have reached a crisis in their relationship and are thinking of calling off the wedding. They've talked it out, and there's just no give on either side on the issue that's troubling them. They think it's time to cancel the wedding.

They may be right, but I'm not so sure. What's happened, from my perspective, is that they have exhausted their current ways of working things out. They've exhausted what they know. They could go on talking, and they might hit upon a solution, but it's equally possible that they'll get tired of it and quit.

What I need to know is, are they ready to get beyond where they are now? Are they ready to step out into space? This chapter (in our book and in their lives) is about space, and stepping out into space—away from the solid and familiar forms of knowing and fixing things they have used up until now. This is the next step they need to take. They've reached a block, a clogging. Can they take a deep breath, relax themselves a little, and float for a while? Their relationship is screaming, "Give me a break!" Can they dare to do it?

If they can, they will learn a lot from floating. It's what we learned when we did our breathing work a little while ago. We are entering into a different kind of knowing, a kind that is not geared toward fixing things, but toward not fixing them; one that realizes that their life together will not be about fixing. Nor will it be about one of them being right and the other being wrong. It will be about their ability to float together through life realizing that their journey together will lead them to whatever solutions they need. That kind of partnership will stand them in much better stead in facing life than one in which they have to know everything, resolve everything, agree on everything, and have being right as the prize and being wrong as the booby prize.

Look what the various scriptures of different religions tell us, if only we will listen. In the Book of Tobit (a great story well worth looking up; it's in the Catholic Bible), Tobit and Sarah (who do not know each other) are so miserable in their lives that each prays to die. God sees them praying and sends an angel who will restore Tobit's sight, give Tobit's son Tobiah to Sarah as a stable and loving husband, and give both Tobit and Sarah a powerful sense of a divine love that surpasses all understanding.

In the New Testament, a man has been waiting for thirty-eight years for someone to help him into a healing pool so that he can be healed of his paralysis. Jesus comes along, sees him, and asks him if he *wants* to be healed. The man says he has no further resources—no one will put him into the pool.

Jesus heals him. In the *Bhagavad Gita*, the god Krishna tells Arjuna, frightened on the eve of battle, to act without experiencing the fruits of action. It's the same invitation to step out into what we do not yet know.

Over and over again, the sacred scriptures tell us that when we have used all our resources, we may feel like we are floating, but if we agree to loosen our grip on what we know we can find a presence of the divine, who will free us.

That's why space is so important to our journey—why we can't allow ourselves to stay mired in what we know. We're like the paralyzed man who waits for thirty-eight years—we're mired and we can go no further. We have to give ourselves space for something different. Those spaces we allow ourselves are windows that show us a greater space— an inner space, the space of the soul—what the old hymn calls "the wideness in God's mercy." We may feel that we are floating there, when the rest of the world is so *sure* about what we should do or not do or who we should be or not be.

But that's why baths have always been so popular down through the centuries and across the civilizations. There's something about floating that we just can't resist.

Is it possible that our cells as well as our souls know that when we are floating, we are very close to God?

CHAPTER NINETEEN

The Heart of Art

Chaos into Form

I will always remember the shoes of Winston Churchill. Now, I never saw his actual shoes; but when I was a child, my parents took me to the Nelson-Atkins Museum of Art in Kansas City to see the watercolors of the great statesman and speaker. I will always remember his painting of a comfy old pair of shoes. They were "just shoes," but somehow Churchill's heart went into them. He transformed them into wonderful, comfortable things. They felt so alive that I expected their owner to step into them at any minute.

That Churchill painting was my introduction to the world of art. It taught me that great art captures your heart and brings you and the canvas to life. I have never had formal art training, or classes in art history. Indeed, I must confess to attending as a child an exhibit of modern art at a university gallery and embarrassing my mother by dissolving into an uncontrollable fit of laughter at the paintings! What a difference between that art and what I had seen of Churchill's!

In the long run, though, I didn't feel so bad about my peals of laughter at the modern art exhibit. Several weeks later, my mother ventured to take me to the same exhibit with the wife of a colleague of my father's who was visiting from suburban Chicago. I was duly warned to be careful, because Mary Anne (or whatever her name was, I forget) was very knowledgeable in the arts and she would be highly offended if there were to be any repeat performance of hilarity on my part. Mary Anne came, and was escorted to the gallery by my mother. She stood in front of the very painting that did me in. Guess what? At the sight of the painting, she, too, dissembled into gales of uncontrollable laughter. My aesthetic instincts were vindicated!

Mary Anne, God bless her, happened to concur with my opinion of that particular painting. Though you and I may disagree as to what is good or bad art, when we see a particular work of art as good, it is because it touches our hearts and connects them to the heart of the artist. Artistry of all sorts transforms our hearts and renews them.

Good or bad art is art, after all, and it engages us. My artistic tastes have matured considerably since the tender days of my youth. When I go through the Metropolitan Museum, the Frick, or one of the private galleries here in New York (such as Ira Spanierman's intimate and inspiring gallery), I am touched by what I see. Whether I fall in love with a particular painting or walk quickly by, it touches me.

What happens is what the philosopher John Dewey called "an experience." Dewey believed that when we are touched by beauty, that moment is very different from the usual run of experiences that we have in life. It sweeps us up and grabs us at the very depths of our being in a way that is important and memorable. Whereas many of the other enjoyable things in life carry with them a reason for our enjoying them, the aesthetic experience, Dewey felt, is truly enjoyment for its own sake, requiring nothing else to validate it.

I agree with Dewey. And, by the way, what he says about the impact of the aesthetic was just as true of the art I saw in the university gallery as it was of the painting of Churchill's shoes. Though I was more appreciative of the latter art than of the former, both swept me away, each in a very different manner. To that degree, both were successful works of art.

Why does this happen, this sweeping away? Some of it has to do with the nature of art. Art is a form of communication, but exactly what is it that art seeks to communicate? "Well," we might say, "art communicates reality." But what exactly does that mean? Does it communicate objective reality, or does it communicate the feelings and impressions of the artist?

When I was in the Jesuit novitiate in Florissant, Missouri, the esteemed Jesuit teacher, theatrical producer, and actor Father John Walsh taught a wonderful course called "God

and Man [it was still the 1960s] in Contemporary Literature."
John Walsh was the sort of person who was not about to let
a course title keep him from covering whatever he wanted to
cover. So, to our great delight, in addition to exploring literature, he took us into the worlds of theater, music, and art.
(Wonders abounded—he even got me to play the lead in a
production of *The Hasty Heart*. Move over, Ronald Reagan.)

Still very active and involved in theater and religious work
to this day, John Walsh has a gift for taking what is complicated and making it understandable. He does it in such a way
that you're left believing there's no other way to think about
it. In fact, you're a bit breathless from the trip from uncer-
tainty to absolute, irrefutable certitude. Perhaps that is why
his classes have stayed with me after three decades.

One of the many valuable things I learned from John
Walsh seems so obvious when I reflect on it today, but it's
really quite brilliant. "Art," he taught us, "tends toward photography or geometry." As I write, I am looking at a repro-
duction of *Salisbury Cathedral from the Bishop's Garden* by John
Constable. All of life is gathered around the cathedral. Ivory
pure, it spires up toward the heavens, whose billowy clouds
and soft blue are mirrored in the pond below. There are animals—cattle graze in the nearby fields and drink from the
reflecting stream. There is vegetation—grasses for grazing
and wonderful spire-like trees that echo the upward stretch
of the church. There are people—a lady and a gentleman,
and the latter's walking stick adds to the heavenward motion

of the church and the trees. I love this piece, and I love to look at it, because it calms me. Everything is in perfect order, "picture perfect" as we say, and we would recognize Salisbury Cathedral from a photograph or if we went there.

By way of contrast, thanks to the Internet, I am now looking at a remarkable painting by Picasso, *Paysage Mediteraneen*, done in 1952. I love this work as much as I do Constable's, but for entirely different reasons. In the house and ship and ocean lie a riot of geometric designs, reds, yellows, greens, oranges. As in Constable's painting, there are blues and whites of sky and ocean, and the upward turns of trees, but here they are abstract and juxtaposed, rather than calmly integrated. Whereas I would look at Constable for calm on a harried day, I would look at Picasso when things were too calm, on days when I found myself slipping into the dull and ordinary. As John Walsh would tell me, you couldn't escape the geometry of this painting if you tried. Art takes the goings-on of the heart and embraces them.

∞

Is there a logic to what goes on in art, something that the mind can get and apply to the state of the heart at any given moment? Of course, there's a simplistic aspect to the John Walsh photography/geometry analysis. No photographer really records objectively—there's always some feeling being conveyed in the light and shadows of a photograph. But it gives us a general idea of what might go on when an artist puts brush to canvas. There's some photography and some geometry in every work of art, and the relative proportion of photography or geometry in every work of art will either confirm our view of life, give us a place of refuge when ours has crumbled, or completely blow our minds.

Sometimes works of art give us comfort. I'm looking at a large watercolor of a country house that hangs in my office. The house is surrounded by a soulful stone wall, gorgeous gardens, and verdant lawns. It even has a footpath. When I'm tired or stressed, I love to sit back and lose myself in those gardens. Nothing about that painting challenges or upsets me. It's my spa, my place of refuge when I need reviving.

Then there is art that we turn to in times of crisis. This art gives shape to life at times when our lives may have lost theirs. "One thing that makes art different from life is that in art things have a shape . . . it allows us to fix our emotions on events at the moment they occur, it permits a union of heart and mind and tongue and tear." The writer and critic Marilyn French wrote these words in 1977 in *The Women's Room*. I think she truly captures a major part of the reason art touches our hearts so deeply when we're in crisis. There is an allure about art that is like an experience of déjà vu. It reminds us of something, yet we can't quite grasp what that something is. Even in a straightforward and realistic painting like Constable's, the realism of the painting leads us to something beyond the cathedral and its pastoral surroundings. It's even more pronounced in Picasso—each part of the painting is a unit in itself and yet somehow works toward a unified whole. It's not anything tangible, but it's something.

That's very different from life. In life, we do not always get the sense that "things have a shape," as Marilyn French puts it. When life deals us a blow, we feel that our lives are without shape or form. In a mid-life crisis, we feel we are wandering around without meaning. In fact, all the talk we have heard for decades now about life being meaningless speaks to this very issue. The word *meaning* itself connotes a middle. The mean is the average, the middle point, of something. When we ask, "What does that statement mean?" we are asking, "What is the point of demarcation that brings it all together?" When we say our life is without meaning, we are saying that it has no point, that there is no grounding point to bring it together. A meaningless statement is one in which the words are all there but nothing unites them. There is a certain kind of brain disorder in which the patient is capable of recognizing words but not of holding them together in a sentence. A meaningless life is like that—there are incidents and memories, but no way of linking them.

We turn to art in times of crisis because it puts some form into the chaos of our lives. On one level, our interest in art is about escaping, but mostly it is about escaping into another world where there is at least some sense, some shape, some meaning. Whether a sculpture or a painting presents a photographic or geometric form, at least it is a form. When we are longing for sense and meaning, we turn to art to find it.

I've been using the word *art* here in terms of painting and sculpture. The term can be applied to literature, theater, music, dance, and architecture as well. Churchill, our friend with the slippers, commenting about architecture, once told *Time* magazine, "We shape our buildings: thereafter they shape us." That's true of all art. Marshall McLuhan said something similar—"The medium is the massage" (yes, that's spelled correctly)—in describing our means of communication. We patronize the arts (hopefully not patronizingly) and we create them because they help us to make sense of things when things just don't make sense. One of the intriguing things about art is that, even when it is abstract and chaotic, it gives us a handle on life that often life itself does not give us.

Sometimes, when it does that, it blows our minds. I'm thinking of the first time my mother, a devout and conservative Roman Catholic, went to her parish church for a weekday Mass, only to find that it was a guitar Mass. It's a stretch to say that the child who was playing the guitar was an artist, but the musical genre my mother encountered sent her into a religious tailspin that would affect her for the rest of her life. Brought up to believe that religious music consisted of organ music and Gregorian chant, she simply could not comprehend what was happening to her or to her church.

Of course, whoever authorized the guitar Mass that Friday morning didn't know my mother and certainly didn't intend to jar her. Sometimes, though, art is created deliberately to shock or at least with the knowledge that it likely will prove shocking to many.

The logic of art is that it either eases or blasts us into a worldview different from our own. Art is a bit of photography and a bit of geometry all rolled up into one. It's objective and subjective all at once. It takes our hearts and asks them what they think reality is.

To this point, I have been using the words *art* and *artist* to mean what we usually mean—something beautiful created by someone who is gifted at expressing beauty in a medium. There's another meaning to the word *art*, however, that I think truly expresses how the soul enters into the world of art.

When we speak of art, we often refer not the work itself, but the know-how that is employed in producing or doing something. Years ago, Erich Fromm wrote a classic book called *The Art of Loving*, in which he taught us how to live a life of love. The Dalai Lama wrote a book called *The Art of Happiness: A Handbook for Living*, which told us what he thought we needed to know in order to live well. There are a couple of stores here in New York City that bear the name "The Art of Shaving." There people can buy fine razors and other accoutrements for depilation.

When we speak of "the art of" something, we have crossed over into the land of soul. My dictionary says that in this sense of "art" we delineate principles for doing something, but I don't think that's entirely accurate. Art in the sense of "the art of" is not so much about principles, I think, as it is about wisdom, savvy, know-how. You can have the principles at your disposal, but without the know-how, you end up with something predictable and wooden.

I've never been much of a painter. I've tried a few times, and I've enjoyed it, but nothing ended up on the canvas that I would consider art. I could probably find a book that would give me some rules for what kind of canvas to use, how to hold the brush, what kind of paint to use, and what strokes to use to apply it. If I followed those rules, my canvas might look better, but I doubt that I would have art. To be an artist, I would have to practice until I got beyond the rules and the lessons and developed the spirit of an artist.

It's the same with being a talk show host. Lots of us in the radio world have written books that, at least in part, describe our work and how we do it. An aspiring host could read those books and try to follow their suggestions, but still not have what it takes to sit behind a microphone. There's an art to it that just has to catch fire from within.

That's when the soul enters into what you do. It takes the technique and transforms it, infuses it with life, and brings out the inner essence and spirit of the artist. The phrase from *A Chorus Line* probably describes the experience as well as any: "God, I'm a dancer!"

When that happens, art has reached its finest hour. Paintings, radio programs, and dance steps all might improve as years go on, but now the soul is there.

You know when you have crossed that threshold into art and soul. You suddenly realize that you're not just writing books—you're a writer. I don't think I quite knew what I was doing when I wrote *Good News for Bad Days*. I was blessed to have Mel Parker (then at Warner) and Denise Marcil, my literary agent, to guide me. By the time I started writing *Stages of the Soul*, I detected a subtle shift: I *knew* how to write a book. Now I find myself writing everywhere—on buses and trains, in free moments in the office or at home. I'm a writer. It's what I do.

Once you know you're an artist from the depths of your soul, it changes your relationship to your mind. You continue to use the principles of your trade, but now you command them instead of their commanding you. Barbara Sher, in *How To Live the Life You Love*, talks about a violinist friend of hers who was practicing the violin in Barbara's house because her own house was being painted. She was playing the most beautiful piece that Barbara had ever heard, and Barbara complimented her. She was surprised when her violinist friend told her that she had been playing the scales! She was so much a violinist that she was able to let her spirit soar through that routine practice piece and turn it into a thing of exquisite beauty. That's when you're really an artist.

Being an artist in this full sense of the word changes your relationship to your heart as well. You love what you do, even on the days when you hate doing it. Not every radio broadcast is a gem, but I still love doing radio. Not every writing session is a fluent, creative moment, but I still love to write. When you grasp and are grasped by the art of something, you are no longer so controlled by your feelings as you once were. You broadcast when it's fun and when it's boring. You write when it flows and when you're blocked.

In the final analysis, what you are grasped by is the divine. There's a story in the Hebrew Bible about the day the Lord told the prophet Jeremiah to go to the potter's house, where he would receive a message. Watching the potter work, Jeremiah saw him create something, then destroy it and make something else. The Lord told Jeremiah that he was going to do the same thing to his people—if they strayed from him, he was going to have to remake them.

That story bothers some people. They resent being told that God is the potter and they are the clay. They want to be the potter—after all, doesn't God want us to work to make the world better?

The answer is, before a potter can make something truly beautiful, he has to be transformed by the art of pottery. He has to become a *potter*. Unless that happens, something important and grand will be missing in the work. When it happens, he will create masterpieces. By the same token, we have to be transformed by God from within before we can effectively do his work of transforming the world. When we find that transformation into "the art of" taking effect in one or more areas of our life, we have encountered the divine; we have been touched by God.

CHAPTER TWENTY

Big Hearts

Sorrow That Expands the Heart

How big is a heart that is "as big as all outdoors"? It is as big as outer space, I guess; and the enormity of the space can sometimes be devastatingly cavernous. I don't think you realize the size of your heart until you feel something or someone missing who used to be there.

The summer in which I am writing this book is one in which I have lost a number of loved ones who were and are very dear to me. I don't want to dwell inordinately on these losses, except to say that somehow they have made me aware of the size of my heart. With the passing of these dear ones, I have come to a better idea of what parents must go through when their children have grown up and left home. There is an enormous, cavernous space. It's a paradoxical space, though, because it is at once both enormously empty and enormously full. Empty because of what is missing, and full because of all the wonderful memories that are stored away.

The heart is an organ—we all know that. But as I write this chapter, a week after Flicka's and Ned's passings, I am profoundly aware that it is also a space.

The heart space, though inner, has true physical, outer correlatives. It is as important that we grant space to our losses as it is essential that we grant space to our loves. I loved my cat Flicka so much because I made so much time for her. Having made that time, the gap that she leaves is all the larger. Perhaps that is why it was so important that I create a space for her in death. It was the hardest thing I ever did to hold that little body in my arms and bury her. But it was important that I did so, and that I did it in a definite space—out in the garden—and that I create a rock garden over her and around her. I wanted there to be something visible and tangible. It is Flicka's space—and without it, I would not have been able to go on. When Ned Giordano, to whom I have dedicated this book, died, it was important for his wife Linda to see him actually placed in his final resting place in the mausoleum. "I couldn't leave," she told me moments later, "without knowing where he was."

I'm watching myself heal—or begin to—from these deaths, and I'm aware of how much space can heal us. As I write, I'm watching the vast expanse of the Long Island

Sound. The sky today is sunny and blue and, to all appearances, infinite. I am aware how much I need the expansiveness of surf and sun and sky to fill my heart and heal it. On my laptop I am listening to classical music from KANU in Lawrence, Kansas, a station that brought me classical music when I was a boy living in Kansas City. Somehow the distance from there to here creates a sense of home and safety after a shattering week. The distance is expansive, the music is expansive, and somehow they help fill the void in my heart.

It seems the heart space has that paradox about it—the irony of distance and proximity. With great amusement and delight, I am learning to welcome into my heart a gorgeous little kitten named Midnight—a domestic shorthair with ebony fur that looks and feels like velvet, and with bright green eyes that touch my heart with life and mischief. I love her, but would I love her so much had Flicka not prepared my heart? Flicka, though gone, has left a legacy and a void that enable me—and Teddy—to welcome this adorable new creature into our hearts. Flicka is gone—yet here. At the same time and in the same respect, she is present and absent. That seems funny to me—so contradictory of the fundamental principles of logic and of metaphysics. In college, I was told that a thing could not *be* and *not-be* at the same time and in the same respect. Flicka, Ned, and all my departed loved ones no longer exist, and yet they do. They create a void, and yet they create a space. My heart looks at the fundamental philo-

sophical principle I learned so long ago—you can't be and
not-be—and it says, "Oh yes you can!"

∞

Indeed, the heart space has that irony about it, and the mind
knows that when it gives it a moment's thought. The word
space, as we have seen, has equal and opposite meanings. On
the one hand, it denotes emptiness; on the other hand, it
denotes "place"—space that is defined and filled. The true
irony is that there can be no place without space. My beautiful view of the Long Island Sound on a sunny day has meaning and definition only because water and sky and trees and
hills all have their proper place. Without that, all would run
together in a hodgepodge. The violin concerto I am listening to right now makes sense only because the violin and the
trumpets and the reed instruments have their own defini-
tions. Each instrument plays sensibly and beautifully only
because pauses between the notes are written into the com-
position. The spaces between the words I am writing enable
this sentence to have meaning. How could I speak if I had
only one breath—if my breaths were not marked by a pause,
however brief, between inhaling and exhaling? Language
itself depends on such a hiatus. We're uncomfortable when
someone we know runs one word into another at top speed.
"Take a breath," we long to tell her.

    That fact of language leads us to discover something
deeper about our lives. Meaning itself depends on the exis-

tence of spaces. Our lives would have no meaning were there not discrete events to give meaning to it. I look at the stars in the New England sky at night, and I know that their mysterious beauty depends not only on them, but also on the vast, dark expanses of night that separate them. It's the same with life. How could we manage our lives if we could not divide them into days and weeks, months and years? How could we come to terms with our growth if we weren't able to divide our lives into phases such as infancy, adolescence, young adulthood, middle age, and old age? "Good fences make good neighbors," Robert Frost tells us—perhaps a bit tongue-in-cheek, but there's truth in his words nonetheless. Without the gaps, the spaces, how could we know or appreciate anything?

Stop to think about it. The times in our lives when we fail to recognize the gaps are often among the most confusing and painful of times. Look at how we live. A couple of years ago, I was working from very early in the morning, then going to the office where I spent the day, then giving speeches or attending meetings by night—and starting the cycle all over again the next day, seven days a week. There were no spaces in my life—every moment was filled. I wondered why I was cranky and exhausted and why I wasn't enjoying life. I needed to—and did—establish gaps in my schedule, evenings and days into which no work-related activity could tread. My life became infinitely saner and happier. I needed my pauses, my space.

It's not just true for me. It's true for all of us. When people become chronically depressed, it becomes hard for them to see any break in the burdens of life. People who are manic can find no break in the euphoria. In the spring and summer of 2000, when several of my loved ones died, I needed to give myself the break of prayer, friendship, play, and nature in order to keep away from a downward spiral.

Spaces give our lives meaning—and bring sanity to our minds and hearts.

I first encountered the notion of *sacred space* when I was in the seminary, learning liturgy and the celebration of religious services. Primarily, it meant that the places in which we encounter God are different from the other places in our lives. That's why we have churches, synagogues, and mosques, places especially designated for divine worship. God can certainly be encountered in ordinary places, but these special spaces allow the break we need from our regular activities and experiences and focus us instead on what is transcendent and divine.

Secondarily, however, sacred space meant the placing of religious objects within a house of worship so as to create an inward sense of balance and peace. There's an art to creating a reverential house of worship. Speaking from my Roman Catholic experience, I can see the differences among churches as to how conducive they are to worship. It's a tricky thing. Some modern Catholic churches are so devoid of religious objects (candles, statues, and the like) as to seem barren and cold, while others seem cluttered with devotional objects. Instinctively, you know when you walk into a church whether it carries with it a sense of the divine. The arrangement of altar, pulpit, tabernacle, candles, crucifixes, and religious images either allows for a congenial space for prayer or it does not. But space is the key—space in which to encounter God.

Hinduism speaks of the gap—the still point or place of nothingness in which the divine is experienced. Eastern meditation—now practiced extensively in the West—emphasizes the space between inhaling and exhaling as a point of encounter with the divine. Western theological tradition holds a place for what it calls "the negative way"—the realization that if we want to know God we must deny the ordinary categories of our experience. In this frame of reference, to say that God is "not good" means that God's goodness is infinitely above our definition of goodness. To know God's goodness we have first to deny it—in effect creating a space or gap between our understanding of goodness and the divine reality.

If that sounds too theologically highfalutin, just realize that this is precisely what happens when our hearts have been broken by life and we are angry with God. We look at the ruins of our lives and say, "God cannot be good if he permitted such devastation to happen to me." We do not yet see that in denying the goodness of God, we are opening the door to seeing a goodness and purpose that are infinitely higher than what we presently know.

Learning that may take a while, a long while. That's the work of the soul—coaching our hearts in the gradual realization that what we think we know may be less important than what we don't know or understand. And that, in turn, our lack of understanding may be the doorway to an inner knowing of the real ways of life and love.

To foster that realization requires space—heart space, mind space, and soul space. It requires emptying yourself of what you think you know and allowing yourself to know things that are beyond your reckoning. Life empties us, and when it does we hate the experience. We grieve, just as I am mourning my friends I lost this spring and summer. But if I can learn to let them go, I will find a whole new treasure and I will truly see the real legacy they have left me. It's these treasures that expand our hearts.

What will Teddy and I come to find in this adorable new kitten, Midnight? If we can let Flicka go, we will discover that she has opened our hearts to love again—and better. Big-hearted people are those whose hearts have been expanded by life. If we are patient and open, we will find in Midnight the mystery of new life, which is Flicka's legacy to us. And we will find, behind it all, the eternal promise and power of the Love that is God.

As I feel my heart being expanded by the deaths of my loved ones, I sense that God is not asking me to remain feeling empty and alone. I am reminded of the time my uncle and aunt decided to expand their house, which required tearing down walls and raising the roof. Unless they did that, they could not have the extra room they needed. My uncle and aunt were the sort of people who loved to have people over—the more the merrier. With five kids, there was never a shortage of people at their house. Tearing down the walls allowed more people to come. In this summer when so many walls have been torn down in my heart, I am grateful to Uncle Jerry and Aunt Bernice for their example. What feels like empty space right now can lead to an expansion of my heart, making room for more people to enter.

CHAPTER TWENTY-ONE

The Heart of God

The Heart of Mystery

"God and I are not on speaking terms." This statement was not a joke. It came from a middle-aged professional woman who felt her life was in shambles. In the blink of an eye, she had lost both her job and her health—and for the first time in her life, she didn't know what to do.

What troubled her most was not the job or the health problems, difficult though they were. What bothered her most was the fact that she had been so devoted to God. Deeply religious, she believed that if she did what was right, prayed, and lived a good life, God would take care of her. She thought that God loved her. She saw herself as his devoted follower and daughter. Why had he let her down?

I hear this sort of thing often, from people of various walks of life. It may surprise you to know that I hear it from the clergy of many faiths as well. Many of them have given themselves totally to God—accepting long hours, meager salaries or stipends, and shouldering the burden of people's pain, anger, and sorrow. Sometimes these men and women of the cloth become so discouraged, it breaks my heart. Sometimes the issue is mistreatment or simple lack of appreciation by superiors. In other cases they are abused or even slandered by those to whom they ministered. In still other cases, they have suffered from painful divorces, the death of a child, or loss of personal health. Why, they wonder, has God not protected them? For years they have told their congregations that if they lived good lives, God would care for them in return. Now they wonder whether they have been fooling themselves and their followers.

The question comes up frequently with my radio callers, who ask about the role of God in the Holocaust. If God is so loving, they ask, why didn't he prevent the destruction of millions of Jews and Christians in the concentration camps? One caller recently put it even more strongly: why should he believe that a God like that even exists?

Along similar lines, a caller questioned me about my own belief. Would there be anything, he wondered, that would so shake my own faith that I would cease to believe in God? I said that I didn't think so, because I had already had a number of earth-shattering incidents in my life and that God helped me to get through them and led me to new and better things. I said that, given this background, I would face a new crisis with that mind-set (or heart-set).

In answer to his question, I also spoke about my life purpose. I told the caller that one aspect of my belief in God was my sense of having a life purpose. In my own case, I describe my mission as "touching hearts to make the world a better place." It seems to me that whatever the crisis, I could still fulfill that mission in some way. That fact bolsters my belief in God, who will always be there to help me.

The problem of the heart of God is much more than a theological or theoretical problem with people: it is a practical one. Many believe that God did not step in to help them when he could have, or promised to.

A common reaction to the ways of God's heart is to assume that God is punishing you for some reason. *If only I had been kinder to my parents, had studied harder, hadn't wasted the early years of life, everything would be fine. But I didn't, and now God is punishing me.* At first, this seems to cast the blame away from God and onto the individual, and to a degree that is true. However, what usually happens is that the person puts the blame right back onto God again. *Why is God such a punishing God? Why does he single me out for punishment when lots of other bad people get off scot-free? Will God, who is supposed to be loving, ever let me off the hook, ever forgive me for the bad things I have done?* We're back to square one again, with reference to the heart of God.

This is how a good many people view the heart of God. As a result, they approach God with fear and trepidation, even with loathing. Like my friend, they are no longer on speaking terms with God.

∞

The Bible, I thought, would be an excellent source for coming to terms with the problem of the heart of God. I was surprised to see that there is nothing said directly about the heart of God in Scripture. A search for the phrase "the heart of God" in the King James and the New International Version of the Bible yielded only two hits (both in the King James). In Ezekiel 28, verses 2 and 6, God tells the prophet to advise the prince of Tyrus that destruction is near "because thou has set thine heart as the heart of God." That's more about idolatry than a revelation of the nature of God's heart.

I find that fascinating, because it is not unreasonable to expect the Bible to tell us about the heart of God. In fact it does, indirectly—it speaks of God's jealousy, his wrath, his mercy, his love. It tells us, "God is love." The Bible assigns to God all of the feelings that we experience as human feelings, except more so, since he is the supreme being.

I think the reason for the indirect approach to God's heart is that at its root, the heart of God is a mystery that we encounter indirectly through the graces bestowed on us, and in the myriad ways in which he presents himself in our everyday lives. In the Hebrew Bible, the heart of God is portrayed as alternately jealous, loving, concerned for the freedom and well-being of his people, vengeful, solicitous that his people return to him, and helpful in the defeat of their enemies. In the New Testament, St. John's writings repeatedly remind us that "no one has ever seen God."

To Christians, Jesus, the Son of God, represents the heart of God, both in his public life on earth and, in the centuries afterward, through the Church. Representing his heavenly Father, Jesus demonstrates a deep sense of divine compassion and mercy. There are frequent references to Jesus' compassion for the crowds, who were "like sheep without a shepherd." His miracles evidence a sense of divine concern for people's material needs, but always with an accompanying concern for their souls. For example, it was not enough for him to multiply the loaves and the fish; he was also concerned that people understand they had the bread of life available for their souls. He could be strict in enforcing the moral law (such as the law about divorce), yet compassionate toward and forgiving of those who broke it (such as the woman caught in adultery). He could enjoy the company of sinners, entering through their doors and leading them through his own. Yet he had no patience for the self-righteous and could address them only to scoff at their pretentiousness. He suffered the unbearable pain of crucifixion while uttering, "Father, forgive them, for they know not what they do."

That the heart of God manifests itself in so many ways should not surprise us after such an extensive study of our own hearts. If our hearts have so many aspects, God's has infinitely more. Hinduism takes the matter further, having God appear in many different personal guises, or *avatars*. If the heart of God is the ultimate unity, it is also the ultimate diversity.

If there are presumably so many diverse and apparently conflicting things in the heart of God, it seems we are left with a problem. How do we reckon with a God whose actions and attitudes of heart can sometimes seem anything but compatible with kind and loving purposes?

It's not a new problem, by the way, or one unique to Judaism and Christianity. The Greeks and Romans had the problem in ancient times, not with one god, but with each of their many gods. Many of the gods, it seems, had dark sides as well as happy, light ones. Listen to what Edith Hamilton wrote in her classic work *Mythology*. Writing of Apollo, the archer god who was also the god of healing, Hamilton notes, "Two ideas were fighting in him as in all the gods: a primitive, crude idea, and one that was beautiful and poetic" (p. 31). The gods have two sides. Indeed, Aphrodite, who is the goddess of love and beauty, is sometimes depicted as weak, and at other times malicious. Hermes was Zeus' trusted messenger and an incorrigible trickster. Diana, the huntress, patroness of hunters, and protector of the young, refused to let the Greeks sail to Troy until a maiden had been sacrificed in her honor. Zeus, the supreme ruler, had a lightning bolt that could strike at will. The problem of dealing with the conflict of the divine heart is clearly not a new one.

Scanning Hamilton's work for a clue to resolve the conflict in the heart of God, I found one in a reference she made to the Greek poet Hesiod. Writing in the ninth century before Christ, Hesiod, the author of *Works and Days* puts forth this remarkable idea: "Fishes and beasts and fowls of the air devour one another. But to man, Zeus has given justice. Beside Zeus on his throne Justice has her seat" (p. 14).

Justice holds a seat next to God, says Hesiod. "Your throne, O God, will last for ever and ever; a scepter of justice will be the scepter of your kingdom," says the psalmist of the Hebrew Bible (Psalm 45:6). Jesus Christ sits at the right hand of the Father, says the New Testament (Romans 8:34). It is the concept of justice that can help us to reconcile the apparent contradictions in the heart of God. For justice means bringing balance to life—giving to everyone his or her due. In Greek mythology, when Zeus observes that Demeter will not allow earth to blossom and that Persephone, from whom she has been separated, is pining away in Hades, he at length steps in and works out a scheme for their reunion sixth months out of each year. When the human race offends God, God sends rain to destroy the earth, but promises Noah that he will never do that again. The Father sends his Son to heal the breach caused by the sin of Adam and Eve.

The mind, it seems, can never fully understand what it finds to be the dark side of the heart of God. But the stories of God assure the mind that, through justice, balance in the world's affairs will ultimately be restored.

That can give a person a great deal to hope for. You may hope for it before you actually believe in it, but it's still a great deal to hope for. One of the things we have learned from the modern fascination with herbal medicine (something that aboriginal peoples knew, but we forgot) is the importance of balance in our bodies. That's what today's homeopathic products often do—restore balance to our systems and thus cure infections and other diseases. We also know the importance of mental balance. When someone is mentally disturbed, we sometimes say that he or she is "unbalanced." We look for ways to restore the person's ability to look at life in a reasonable way.

What may be strange is the notion that justice is about balance. It is, really; for justice is giving to everyone what is due to him or to her. If someone fails to give you due credit for your work on a project, trying to take credit for it—something is unbalanced, and the balance needs to be restored. That is the concept behind legal justice: scales that balance evenly. Alexander Pope's "Poetic Justice, with her lifted scale, where, in nice balance, truth with gold she weighs, and solid pudding against empty praise" ("The Dunciad," I, 52) speaks the same about poetry. In our human works and in our lives, our minds look for justice, and we see the establishment of justice, of course, as a human endeavor, but also as a work of the gods, of God. Believing people tend to assume that God will right all wrongs, even though we give him a bad review if his justice falls heavily upon our own shoulders. Or if, in our opinion, the benefits of his creation of balance fail to benefit our lives enough. Poor God.

∞

The mind hopes for justice from the heart of God, but the soul takes us somewhere else. For the soul, justice is not about adding quantities or measures to one or the other side of a balancing scale. That is problem solving. For the soul, justice is the mysterious fulfillment of two powerful desires—on the one hand, the desire of our heart to mingle with God's, and on the other, the desire of God's heart to mingle with ours.

Is the heart of God a problem—or a mystery? Both are instances of the coexistence of unity and complexity. Ordinary thought and speech do not lead us to realize that problems and mysteries are different, but they are. "What am I going to do about my teenage son? It's a mystery." No, it's a problem. If it becomes a mystery, that's actually good news.

The word *problem* comes from a Greek word meaning "to throw forward." *Mystery*, on the other hand, is commonly thought to derive from Greek words meaning "a secret rite" or "an initiate." But sources indicate that it further derives from a Greek word meaning "to close one's eyes."

It's helpful to play with this for a moment. A problem—or, we could say, a *puzzle*—is something that is hurled into our lives and that we try to resolve with our eyes open. I can't close my eyes and solve a Sunday *New York Times* crossword puzzle. I'd better have my eyes wide open if I've said

something to offend someone and I'm trying to figure out
how to take my words back. Those are puzzles or problems.

Mysteries are different. Inherent in the Greek word *mys-
terion* is the sense that the puzzle is not outside us, but rather
that we and life together are the puzzle, that the proper
approach to solving it is with one's eyes closed and one's focus
turned inward. Trying to come to terms with the loss of a
beloved spouse is very different from solving a whodunit. It
involves us—turns us inside, right where we live. The "it"
here is the nature of life and death, the very nature of life
itself. When Dad lost my mother to cancer after forty years
of marriage, it was the death-dealing nature of life that shattered his heart. It wasn't a question, as we so often claim, of
"putting the pieces of his life back together." It was, rather,
a question of dealing with the stark realization that living is
about dying, joy about sorrow, and loving about saying good-
bye. In times of mystery we bond with life and life bonds
with us in a moment of mutual self-revelation. When both
we and life (we and God, I say) reveal ourselves at a moment
when each is not at its loveliest. The heart of God seems
cruel—why couldn't Mom have been spared? Our heart is
dazed and bewildered and maddened.

Sometimes we resolve the situation by walking away for
a while. A friend of mine, now a devout believer, walked
away from God for seven years after the stillbirth of her child.
Sometimes we need to do that. But when we're ready to let
the mystery be what it is in all its unloveliness, remarkably we

come to a partnership with life, with God, that goes beyond our acceptance or nonacceptance of the tragedy and tells us instead from deep within our hearts and souls that our lives have a purpose and that we have an ultimate partner who wants nothing more than to love us as we fulfill that purpose. Dad never recovered fully from the loss of my mother, but he found peace with God and ways to be a friend and helper to others. My friend who lost her baby now helps others through the gift of healing, and brings them to God. What I said to my radio caller is true: with a life purpose forged in the white heat of life experience, you can withstand anything and unite your heart with the heart of God.

The truth about the heart of God is that it wants nothing more than to know us, to love us, and to serve us in this life and to be happy with us in the next. Roman Catholics will see that statement as the inverse of a statement made in the Baltimore Catechism, which we may have memorized back in our grammar school days. In answer to the question, "Why did God make us?" we learned, "God made us to know, love, and serve him in this world and to be happy with him in the next." For us, who are made in the image and likeness of God, the Baltimore Catechism's statement about *our* purpose on earth gives us a powerful statement about God's purposes as well. The question inherent in our hearts is, Can we allow that love, and will we return it?

Letting the heart of God be a mystery—not in the sense of a distant, remote, and unknowable thing, but in the sense of something that involves us—allows us to see both God and ourselves in a different light. If God wants to know, love, and serve us, and if we want to know, love, and serve God, then we are working together with God for each other and for the betterment of the world. We don't always see eye to eye, God and us—but do we always see eye to eye with anyone? If we know that God wants the best for us, and if we know that we want the best for God, and that we both want the best for the world, then there is a great deal that we can accomplish, even when we do not understand one another.

It seems to me that this makes our relationship with God very real. It's kind of like the relationship we might have with a family member whom we may not always understand, but who is always family. Isn't it interesting, too, to think of God looking at us that way? We often think of ourselves as so perfect, when we're angry with God—we're perfect and God is flawed. What if God in those moments looked at us with loving curiosity and said, "I don't especially like this person right now, but I love him because he's family." Could it work both ways?

The problem of God's heart is really a mystery, and the problem of our divided hearts is really a mystery, too. There are different ways to experience it, different ways to understand it. But in the final analysis it's a familial bond, which, rather than requiring full agreement, is able to embrace disagreements about works and ways, and, in the final analysis, just "be family."

CHAPTER TWENTY-TWO

Hearts That Remember,
Hearts That Live

"Ask not for whom the bell tolls. It tolls for thee." Like most young folks in their early twenties, I read those words without a thought in the world that they applied to me. Charles Rogers, professor of my sophomore literature class at Rockhurst University and a truly outstanding teacher of the written and spoken word, warned us that those immortal words about mortality penned by "Dr. Donne the Divine" (as he called John Donne) were meant as food for thought. The clouds of Vietnam were looming large over our horizons, and I suppose Donne's words should have been an omen to us. But we were still the sons of innocent days, and we blithely tucked those words into our memories for exam time and headed blissfully to the Rock Room for a Coke or a coffee.

How time changes the heart. In the nearly forty—
egad!—years since I first heard Donne's words, I have been
near death myself and have participated in the funerals of my
parents, students, friends, colleagues, and countless strangers.
Hearing Donne's words again recently, read on tape by Wayne
Dyer, I found myself sitting bolt upright, stunned by a thun-
derbolt of recognition.

Death never ceases to affect us, though we try valiantly to
put it out of our minds. As I have mentioned, within the past
several months of this writing, I have been deeply affected by
the deaths of some outstanding people I knew very well. It
was on an October Tuesday morning that I arrived at my
office to learn that Monsignor Jeremiah Monahan, the Chan-
cellor of the Archdiocese of New York, had died the previous evening of a heart attack. *How could this be?* I wondered.
I had just seen Jerry, had chatted with him on the elevator.
He looked tired, I thought, but certainly not like a candidate
for death. I had been off the previous day, and had not known
that he had been rushed to the hospital from his office with
chest pains, had rallied a little during the day, and was fatally
stricken that night. All I could think of in the days that followed was Jerry's gentle way, his constant and fatherly appreciation of my radio work, and his quiet but infectious sense
of humor. At his funeral, Cardinal O'Connor—himself
gravely ill—recalled how, without ostentation, Jerry would
prepare the supper trays for their dinner at the Cardinal's res-

idence and equally without fanfare remove them at the end of the meal. That was Jerry. Now he was gone.

The suddenness of Jerry Monahan's death stunned us all. What dominated my own feelings was the realization that we never know when someone we love is going to leave us. I wished there had been time to thank him for his kindness and to let him know how much it mattered. It taught me the importance of loving and appreciating people daily—and letting them know it. If we wait, we may have to wait forever.

Seven months later, Cardinal O'Connor died. It was May 3, and the previous August His Eminence had undergone surgery for brain cancer. He never fully recovered from that and from the effects of his radiation treatments. His death was not unexpected, although every day of his illness I tried to imagine that he would recover and return to us as our vigorous and feisty Cardinal. When he died at 8:05 P.M. on May 3, 2000, I felt as though I had been dealt a blow in the stomach. Just a day before, we had buried Phil. How could this be happening?

By no means was I a member of the Cardinal's inner circle. Yet there was a deeply personal relationship between His Eminence and me that was much like the relationship between a father and a son. We had first met twenty years ago, when Archbishop O'Connor (he was not yet a Cardinal) came to St. Mary's Church on Grand Street to meet with the staff. We were about to replace the pastor, Father Edward

Byrne, who was to begin a tour of duty as a missionary in Latin America. I was still a Jesuit, not yet a priest of the Archdiocese of New York, and was meeting the Archbishop for the first time. For a host of reasons, the meeting was a difficult one. In the middle of the discussion, Archbishop O'Connor stopped and looked me straight in the eye for a full minute, with the most penetrating gaze—it went right through me and out the other side. To this day, I do not know what he was thinking. But I do know that at that moment, a bond was formed between us.

A decade later, when I was thinking about leaving the Jesuits and becoming a priest of the Archdiocese of New York, Cardinal O'Connor was more than gracious and welcoming to me. Though he could sometimes appear to be brusque and businesslike in public, the Cardinal was most gracious in his private meetings, especially with his priests. Every Wednesday was given to meeting priests. Any priest could come, with or without an appointment, and discuss whatever was on his mind. Over the years, I had several of those meetings with the Cardinal, and enjoyed them immensely.

One of my favorite memories of Cardinal O'Connor was his appearance on "As You Think." The interview took place shortly before Christmas of 1997, and I opened by asking him what Christmas was like in the O'Connor household when he was growing up. He rose to the occasion, warmly describing a household in which there was often very little, but always enough to share with anyone in need. Two years later, when (with some nudging from Joe Zwilling, director of the Office of Communications for the Archdiocese of New York) the Cardinal appointed me director of radio ministry, I met him in a reception line where he was greeting employees of the Archdiocese. "Well," he said to me, "here's my new director of radio ministry. Merry Christmas, young man." He always called me "young man." On a busy Sunday morning after his Mass, he always greeted people who came to meet him. When I was on duty, I would stand off to the side of the meeting area outside his sacristy, where he vested for Mass, so as not to interfere. No matter how many people he had to greet, he would manage to catch my eye for a nod or a wave or a handshake.

I'll always remember the cocktail reception he gave in his private office when my book *Good News for Bad Days* was published. A lot of the people who came were somewhat intimidated at meeting him. He immediately put them at ease and made them feel comfortable and welcome. When people asked him to sign copies of my book, he would sign, "John Cardinal O'Connor, the non-author."

I loved the Cardinal. When Jerry Monahan died and I was reflecting on the importance of appreciation, I decided to write to the Cardinal, knowing that he was gravely ill, to thank him for all that he had done for me. Shortly thereafter, I received a note back, deflecting my gratitude and instead expressing his gratitude to me. That was his way.

When the heart is riddled by the deaths of loved ones, memory is the mind's way of helping the heart to cope and to heal. Memory is twofold. On the one hand, it is the bits and pieces—the mental snapshots—that we take along the way and recover only later. And on the other hand, memory is the flow of those events, the unifying energy that makes them something more than mere discrete and unrelated moments from the past. The flow of memory puts them into a whole, and that is truly what enables the heart to heal. Just as energy is both particle and wave, so the memory is the individual remembrances and the flow that holds them together. Generally, I think, we get the discrete memories, and then we get the underlying flow. When the Cardinal died, I began to be in touch with my wonderful memories of him, some of which I have shared with you. Later, those individual moments locked together into an underlying sense of the Cardinal's presence in my life. The memories, I think, are the mind's contributions to the process of healing. The underlying flow of the meaning of them all is the soul's.

In his autobiographical book *A Long Way to Tipperary*, the biblical scholar John Dominic Crossan describes his grief over the death of his wife Margaret. Crossan notes that there was a difference between his public and his private grieving. The public grieving took place over three days and included a wake, a funeral service, and the expressions of sympathy of a host of friends and acquaintances. The private grieving lasted three months, the period of time he had off before resuming his teaching schedule. During this time he painstakingly went through Margaret's clothing and possessions, disposed of them, and began the process of learning to live alone. I am sure his actual grieving period far exceeded three months, but I found his distinction between the public and the private aspects of grief to be illuminating. The longer, private, grieving time was the time for memories and the flow of memory about his life with Margaret, a long, slow time to sort things out emotionally.

The process of remembering the individual moments of a life is a most important one. Even if the memories are painful in part, the very act of acknowledging them helps us with the process of moving on. Here our minds begin to sort out what is in our hearts.

∞

It is not enough to have a box full of snapshots. Sooner or later, the snapshots must be mounted and put into an album, where they have their proper place among the stuff of life. When you have only the memories and not the underlying flow, something important is missing. My paternal grandmother died when I was two years old. I saw pictures of her, viewed her paintings, and heard my father's stories about her, without having any overall impression of her. Recently, after looking at a candy jar of hers that is in my possession, the stories and the memories and the impressions—the snapshots—came together. In an instant, I *knew* my grandmother as a person, had a sense of why she had meant so much to my father, and felt that in the beauty of her spirit, she had contributed greatly to my life as well.

Throughout these chapters of the heartstorming process, I have relied greatly on stories to plumb the rich depths of the heart. Stories provide the mind with its snapshots, and the soul with its depth of tone and color. The snapshots alone do not do it. If I walk into someone's house and see on the mantel pictures of their sons and daughters and grandchildren, I get only a small piece of the relationships that are there. When my host or hostess begins to tell me stories about them, then I can really relate to them.

For years, Nana, my mother's mother, had a farm lady who came on Saturday mornings to sell eggs. Mrs. Marshall was a friendly and talkative woman with the open heart of country people. Whenever Mrs. Marshall would see me at Nana's, she would fairly cackle with tales of Lois Barbara, her granddaughter, who was about my age. She showed me pictures of Lois Barbara, but it was the stories that connected me with her, even though I had never met her. I sometimes wonder what became of Lois Barbara. I'm sure her grandmother told her stories about me. Whenever Mrs. Marshall saw me, she would inevitably say, "My, you're just growin' like a weed." Just before leaving she would promise, "I'm going to tell Lois Barbara I saw you."

I could show you a photograph, if I had one, of Mrs. Marshall. But now you know her, and have a feeling of what it was like for me to know her. Stories do that—they take the snapshots and bring them to life.

The snapshots and the flow, working together, help us to deal with the loss of loved ones and to heal. They bring life and resurrection out of death and loss. There is something about Jerry Monahan, Cardinal O'Connor, Grandmother Keenan, Nana, Mrs. Marshall, and even Lois Barbara, if she's gone, that will never die as long as I am around to tell their stories; and there is something about me that will never die as long as there are people around to tell mine.

Gulp. Does that mean that someday it really will be over? That day when the last human being has turned out the lights, left the face of the earth, and gone to his or her eternal reward? When there is no one on earth to tell the stories, on that day will my life have become forgotten and pointless?

No, and this is the really good news. It comes in two parts. One, no one who has ever known you will ever forget you. The beauty of the flow of memory is that it contains your snapshots for always. They will go to the eternal reward with anyone who takes them there. (Want proof of that? Have you ever had a snapshot memory of someone or something come to you out of the blue? Where do you think it came from, if not from the flow of memories your soul contains?)

The second part is even better than that. Not only will others take the memory of you with them, God will never forget you: "Shall a woman forget her baby at her breast or fail to cherish the son of her womb? But even if these should forget, I will never forget you" (Isaiah 49:15). Your life, my life, are all part of the flow of the life of God. "Christ plays in ten thousand places, lovely in limbs and lovely in eyes not his," declared the poet Gerard Manley Hopkins, and he is saying the very same thing. Wherever we are or have been, there is a little aspect of the divine life brought into the unity of the whole by the divine attention. One of the big differences between God and us is that there is no inattention in God. He never forgets, he never falls short, he never fails to pay attention to any aspect of his creation. Have you ever been amazed at how the tip of your finger knows how to heal when a part of it is cut? You don't have to pay attention in order to make it heal, but something within the finger is paying attention in ways that we can only wonder at. God is like the tip of our finger. He is always paying attention, always knowing how to make things happen. If you have been here, he will never forget you.

And that's important. Because, in a real way, we will still be around. Perhaps not here on earth, but somewhere else, in the afterlife. Having souls, we don't just go away. With God, we will never have to worry about being recognized. Does that sound foolish? Well, have you ever been at a party or some other gathering and gone up to meet someone who should have known you, but didn't? It's an awful feeling. You feel so insignificant and useless. Whenever I go to a parish or a group where I have been before, people always come up and say, "Do you remember me?" We all want to be remembered.

When we come to meet God, we will never have to worry about being recognized and remembered. He will remember us and know us. Don't let that scare you. God is very positive.

The snapshots of the mind and the flow of memory rescue our lives from the finality we fear about the grave. They truly resurrect us, raise us from the shadow of death. It's true of our own memories of our loved ones as well. "Even though I walk in the valley of the shadow of death," the psalmist says, "I fear no evil. For you are at my side" (Psalm 23:4). When we can honestly say to a fellow human being, "I will never forget you," we are the ones who are at their side, saving them from the shadow of death.

So don't be afraid to grieve. "Blessed are you who mourn," said Jesus, and it is true. Feel free to walk in the valley of darkness, sad over a loved one who has died. Just know that, thanks to you, death is not victorious, but rather is conquered by the glorious rememberability of the soul.

PART III

HEARTSTORMING

IN EVERYDAY LIFE

CHAPTER TWENTY-THREE

The Cry of God

As you can see, the process of heartstorming is very simple. It requires no expensive equipment, no great abundance of time, and no exceptional skills or abilities. It doesn't require a lengthy trial period in order for you to see results. You don't need to be trained in a particular area, and you don't need a graduate or postgraduate degree.

Despite the simplicity and accessibility of the heartstorming process, most of us don't take time to do it. As simple as it is, you would think that it would be the first thing we would think of. Yet most of us don't even know that the process exists.

Why not? The reasons are simple. We all know them, as well as we know the palm of our hand. I call them the "terrible toos." They are the negative attitudes and ideas that keep us defending our limitations and prevent us from over-coming them. As we'll see, they're very similar to the "ter-rible twos" that a toddler and her parents go through in the second year of a child's life. Like a toddler, they can hold us hostage in a tyrannical vise grip. Let's take a look at some of them—they are legion—and see what we allow to be done to ourselves when we'd really *like* to change.

Too Busy   At thirty-five, Bob was running out of steam. A bright, creative idea man, his long hours and dedication had propelled him to the number-two spot in a major commu-nications and information company. "I don't have a life," he complained. "I don't have time to date or play golf or do any-thing fun. I scarcely have time to call my parents and sisters."

Bob was looking for more, and he increasingly felt that he was on a treadmill. His job still stimulated him, but allowed him none of the things in life that he really loved to do.

Bob was ahead of the game in that he knew this about himself. Being an intelligent man and a winner, he should have been a ripe candidate for change, right?

When I suggested to Bob that he do a little heartstorm-ing, he actually flew into a rage. "I don't have time for the stuff I have to do at work. I don't have time to do the laun-dry and clean the house. Where am I going to find time for anything else?" He practically threw me out of his office.

Bob's dilemma is one that many of us recognize. We've all done the same thing—we've maneuvered ourselves into a busy, fast-paced lifestyle, and the lock is on so tight and we've become too busy to get out. Or so we think. "Too busy" is a "terrible too" because it keeps us running and running but not enjoying life.

With this or any other terrible toos, the trick is to work *with* it, not against it. The terrible toos are a way of protecting what we have. Bob needed to protect his career. That was a good motive. The problem was, it was killing him.

In order to get his life where he wants it to be, Bob will need to co-opt that self-protective instinct. To do this, he must learn to stop saying, "I'm too busy to . . ." and simply acknowledge, "I am too busy." When that happens, he will come face-to-face with the reality that the way he is living now is lethal. His desire to protect himself will then kick in and actually get him to make a change. All that the terrible toos care about, really, is that we're safe.

It's amazing what can happen when we take our terrible toos seriously. As I mentioned earlier, there came a point a couple of years back when I discovered that I was working from early morning to almost midnight every day. While I loved my work, I was dragging myself around and felt that I was constantly running from place to place, bus to train to connecting train, falling into bed and getting up again at dawn to start the process all over again. It took me a while to say, "I'm too busy," but once I did I reworked my schedule. I programmed in evenings just for myself, limited the evenings on which I accepted talks or other engagements, and negotiated at the office for two days off a month. I'm still busy, but now I have time for things other than work. It has made a big difference.

Too Tired   Sometimes we really are too tired, and we can stop and do something about it, such as get to bed early for a couple of nights. People with chronic illnesses such as chronic fatigue syndrome are "too tired" most of the time, and the process of rebuilding their physical and spiritual immune systems can provide some help. But when "I'm too tired" becomes a terrible too, our fatigue keeps us from living fully—or even wanting to. I was not only "too busy," but "too tired" to change. It seemed easier to say yes to that extra church service or that talk way outside of town, and so my schedule kept piling up and I felt increasingly draggy and drained. I was, or felt that I was, too tired to change. My terrible too was trying to protect me. It told me how much people needed my message, how good it was to give it so readily, and how people wouldn't understand if I changed. I was too tired to cope with all of that, and it was easier to say yes to everything than to deal with the guilt I would have from saying no. When I finally realized making changes to achieve a more balanced life would be better for me, I did it, and was glad. Having a chance to relax a little, and to have time for things I enjoy, has actually enhanced my work rather than ruined it. Once my terrible too realized that a change would help me, I was able to stop saying, "I'm too tired to change" and instead to say, "I'm too tired." Then I could make some changes.

Too Poor   Every once in a while, I see a bumper sticker that reads, "I owe, I owe, so off to work I go." It's pretty funny, but it also reveals a terrible too. When we get ourselves convinced that we are too poor to make the changes we want to make in our lives, to enjoy life and relieve some of its burdens, we are as much hostages as if we were parents with a child who forever says "NO!" The terrible too thinks it's protecting us from getting in over our heads financially, and so gets us to say "no" to everything. We're too poor to go on vacation. We're too poor to buy a good used car. We're too poor—heaven help us—to enroll in a financial planning seminar or to learn how to invest in the stock market. Besides, if we start tinkering with finances, we might lose our shirt and then be even poorer.

Again, the instinct is a good one: we're protecting ourselves from making things even worse. But we're also protecting ourselves from making things better. Positive change comes only when we stop saying, "We're too poor to . . ." and start saying, "We're too poor." Then the whole dynamic changes. The terrible too then sees that it can better protect us by helping us to do some financial planning and wise investing so that we can do some of the things that we love, all the while learning the art of careful spending. When we get tired of being "too poor," we cease to be tyrannized by our terrible too and begin to see that we need not envision ourselves as poor at all. That can be a tremendous freedom.

Too Underqualified   I was raised to believe that without a Ph.D., I would not amount to anything. Fortunately, I never believed it, even though I started (and gladly left) doctoral studies. A doctorate is a great credential, and once in a while I think of pursuing one again. But people often grind themselves down in the crucible of life by constantly reassuring themselves that they are too underqualified to do something that they truly want to do. "I'm too inexperienced to write a book," I once told myself. "I'm too old to take up golf," a senior friend recently lamented. "I could never learn to become a chef," a young man told me, even though he loved to cook and could certainly pass a culinary course. We love to tell ourselves that we're too underqualified to realize our dreams.

Again, we're protecting ourselves. Our terrible too is screaming "no," because it doesn't want us to try, then fail and get hurt. The turning point comes when we cease to say, "I'm too underqualified to . . ." and simply say, "I feel too underqualified, and I hate it. Let me see what the qualifications *really* are and then find the best way to get the ones that I need." In my own case, I learned that I had all the experience and talent necessary to write not one, but (at this point) four books. Who needs a college degree in writing? Sometimes there are real qualifications that we prefer not to meet, but there may be related things that we might just as happily qualify for. For example, I love to care for animals. While I would not want to get the schooling necessary to be a veterinarian, I would love to learn enough to care for rescued animals. Once we make our terrible too into an ally, our safety then lies in fulfilling our dream, not in avoiding it. Most of us are better qualified than we imagine, and can readily get whatever additional knowledge or credentials we need.

Too Hurt   This is a very common complaint, and it cuts to the heart of the terrible toos. Almost without exception, someone or something has hurt us in the past. It may be, but need not be, outright abuse. Whatever form it took, it left us scarred for life. "I'm too scarred to have a good marriage," a woman once told me. "I was laughed at for wanting to play the piano—I'll never be able to play in public," a middle-aged man recounted. As before, we're simply trying to protect ourselves from getting hurt. When we can stop saying, "I'm too hurt to . . ." and instead acknowledge "I'm too hurt for my own good," we can let ourselves do things we never thought possible. Once it feels safe to fulfill our dreams rather than to abandon them, we will go forward into miraculous lives.

Too Afraid   This terrible too is really at the heart of them all. It's also the one we're least likely to admit to. Whether we're afraid to leave our house, to fly in an airplane, to publish our manuscript, or to make a speech in public, our fears form a terrible too that keeps us from realizing some aspect of ourselves that we would truly love and deeply enjoy. Again, it's a safety factor—an agoraphobic person becomes nervous and can hardly breathe because he senses danger in the world at large. The would-be author is afraid of public criticism and ridicule. The nervous speaker is afraid she will appear a fool. The person who won't fly is afraid of having a fatal accident in the air. As with the other terrible toos, growth can begin when we move from saying, "I'm too afraid to . . ." and simply realize, "I'm too afraid." Once we see that our fears are getting in the way of our living, and that we will be safe if we pursue the things we are afraid of, we can proceed to make this terrible too into an ally for the pursuit of a new adventure.

Too Depressed   From time to time, I meet people who describe themselves as "too depressed" to get out of bed, go to a therapist, go to a party, or visit friends. Depression may happen for a variety of reasons, and we should be careful to avoid harshly judging people who are depressed. A depressed person is trying to protect himself from perceived danger or pain. Depression may be useful for a while: for example, it may incline us to take sufficient time to mourn the loss of a loved one rather than force ourselves to rush back into "normal" life. It becomes a terrible too when we become immobilized by it and lose our ability to participate in life. The turning point for change comes when we stop saying, "I'm too depressed to . . ." and instead acknowledge, "I'm too depressed." Once we make that acknowledgment, we can get help to lessen the depression and, if at all possible, to understand its meaning and move beyond it. Then we can begin to find it safe to see a doctor or a therapist or to take some small steps toward moving out into society. As long as it knows we're safe, the terrible too is more than happy to cooperate in our healing and in the eventual expansion of our life.

∞

The terrible toos are the reasons that people so often fail to make important positive life changes. Heartstorming is the key to our getting free when we are trapped in the terrible toos. The basic process involves co-opting the terrible toos and, instead of allowing them to trap us in negative patterns, transforming them into instruments of safety and freedom.

As we saw, the pattern of transformation is like this:

Stage 1: "I am too _____ (scared, depressed) to _____."

Stage 2: "I am too _____ (scared, depressed)."

Stage 3: "I am safe enough to deal with my _____ (fear, depression) and move beyond it."

The process of heartstorming, too, as we saw, involved three stages:

Stage 1: The heart reacts to a situation.

Stage 2: The mind reflects on what the heart brings and draws an answer, a solution, or an understanding.

Stage 3: The soul draws the impressions of the heart and the understanding of the mind into the ambience of wisdom and the overall purpose of one's life.

Now, let's put this all together. When we are trapped in one or another version of the terrible toos, the process of coming to true freedom involves the heart, the mind, and the soul. Here's what we have:

Heart (Stage 1): "I am too _____ to _____."

Mind (Stage 2): Redefines Stage 1 to "I am too _____."

Soul (Stage 3): Allows me to see that universal value (beauty, peace, wisdom, love, and so on) will be there for me when I change. "I am safe to change."

The process of heartstorming is a helpful way to move from toxic feelings and attitudes that rob us of our dreams. The process of acknowledging our heart's attitudes, reframing those impressions through the mind, and realizing that there are lasting—indeed, eternal—benefits that make it safe for us to change, helps us to rid ourselves of feelings and attitudes that keep us from living as fully as we want to or are meant to.

The second stage, in which the mind reframes what the heart has given it, is a giant step, indeed. It signifies a realization that what has been a rule of life is no longer acceptable. Instead of saying, "This is a horrible situation. I am too weak to change," I now say, "This is a horrible situation that I should consider changing." It's a big thing to go from saying, "I'm too underqualified to leave this dead-end job" to affirming, "I'm underqualified, all right—but I can do something about it."

Instead of saying, "I'm too poor to leave this miserable situation and go for something better," I now say, "I'm poor now, but I have the dreams and resources to make something of my life."

When the mind reframes the old rules given it by the heart, a powerful force for change is unleashed. Now the mind has vision and the heart has hope. The old rules have been declared null and void, and new, more positive rules have replaced them. Now I am free to look at programs, options, and opportunities to make my new vision operative in my life.

All I need now is to know that it is safe for me to do so. That's the fruit of the third stage, in which the soul takes over and helps me to align my newfound willingness to change with a sense of divine purpose and protection. "I can do all things in him who strengthens me," St. Paul told the Philippians (4:13).

"Once I realized that the option of enrolling in graduate school would open more doors than continuing to tell myself I was too stupid, I knew it was the right thing for me to do," said Joan, who had stayed in a low-paying job, believing it was all she could do.

That third step—realizing that it is safe to change—is the one that helps us to put our new vision and new rule into effect.

What's behind this is the phenomenon that safety and purpose go hand in hand. We feel safe when the course of action we are pursuing or intending to pursue has a purpose. We get edgy and nervous when it does not.

What happens often enough is that we make compromises with our safety. We know we're in a job that's going nowhere, and it makes us nervous to be there. But we feel we're too unqualified for a better-paying job and that we're too old or not smart enough to get the schooling needed to move on. It doesn't feel safe to stay, and it doesn't feel safe to move on. Often, we'll convince ourselves that it's safer to stay than to try to get the extra schooling, even though we feel frustrated. Until it feels safe to make the change, we likely won't. It will feel safe when we have a sense that to do so is essential to our purpose and will significantly improve our situation. When I was thinking about leaving the Jesuits and becoming a priest of the Archdiocese of New York, I delayed the decision because I was too scared to make the move. Finally, I talked it over with a priest friend who reassured me and paved the way for me to see Cardinal O'Connor. I came to see that it was the right course of action for me in fulfilling my purpose on earth. I felt safe and went ahead to set the process in motion.

The process of heartstorming is not only helpful for dealing with the terrible toos as we make pivotal life decisions. As I went through it for this book, I was not trying to make sweeping changes, but rather to find a way to experience life more deeply through the eyes of my heart. As you see, I took a number of random aspects of my life and put them through the process. This is very useful for undertaking any kind of creative activity or pondering anything you want to pursue in greater depth. A writer or a painter experiencing a block might make good use of the heartstorming process to get free. It might go something like this:

Stage 1 (Heart): How do I feel about this project right now? Do I feel overwhelmed? Am I afraid I won't succeed with it? Am I afraid that I might succeed, and afraid of what the consequences of that might be? Do I feel overwhelmed? Disinterested? Do I feel pressured by deadlines or expectations, or by financial considerations related to completing it?

Stage 2 (Mind): What's the overall lesson I'm getting from my feelings? If I'm feeling overwhelmed, what would it take to put me back in command of the project? If I'm feeling pressured, what would it take to relieve the pressure? If I'm disinterested, what would it take to get me going again? Or should I put the project on hold and work on something else?

Stage 3 (Soul): Does it feel safe to complete the project? Does the project have a higher purpose for being in my life? When working on it, have I felt inspired or guided?

Heartstorming can also be helpful in working out marriage or other relationship problems. In such situations, communications often fail because the parties are unclear about what they feel, think, and want. They may also have poor communication skills, which is a separate issue. But the best communication skills are useless if the people involved are unclear about what each of them wants.

A heartstorming process to settle a disagreement in a marriage or other relationship might go along the following lines:

Stage 1 (Heart): What do I feel about this issue? What does my spouse (or friend) feel? What are the similarities and differences in our feelings? (Possible feelings include passion, anger, indifference, fear, humor, and so on. Name the feelings—don't evaluate them as good or bad just yet.)

Stage 2 (Mind): Are we on each other's side or on each other's back? If we're on each other's back, can we learn to appreciate the truth in the other's position? If we're on each other's side, but disagree, can we affirm what might be useful in the other's point of view? Can we talk about the differences in our viewpoints and learn something from each other? Are there points on which we may amicably agree to disagree? If we are on each other's back rather than on each other's side, do we see that this is not good either for us individually or for our relationship? Can we pledge—not try, but pledge—to turn it around?

Stage 3 (Soul): Here we go back to the very beginning of our relationship and recall what brought us together in the first place. In most relationships, the beginning moments are marked by a sense of magic or destiny. Perhaps we were attracted to each other instantly. Or maybe it took a while. When the magical moment came, we felt that there was a special bond between us, whether a bond of friendship or of love. It was meant to be. After a while, especially in a marriage, the sense of being destined to be together forever can disappear. Let's face it—when we're using our mind to work on our marriage, there will be times when the various methods we try will not appear to be working. If we can recall that original sense that we were meant to be together, we can find ourselves compelled to "try, try again," because we sense that our relationship is part of our purpose here on earth. Something is not quite right if we don't try again.

Sometimes a married relationship does not begin with a sense of destiny but develops one later. Perhaps the marriage was arranged without the consent of the partners. Or, more likely today, there was some other factor—perhaps an unexpected pregnancy—that hastened the entry into marriage. As time goes on, the couple may realize that their coming together was no coincidence. Rather, they became aware that Love's intention, and not coincidence, brought them together in marriage. Should this sense, in turn, fade with time, remembering those moments of the realization of the mystery of Love's ways can help restore the life of the marriage.

∞

This heartstorming process as applied to marriage can be used by both partners together or by one partner alone who wants to save a troubled marriage. Especially when one begins to restore a troubled marriage alone, the soul's input—the sense of the rightness or destiny or purpose of the marriage—is of tremendous importance. It is the why that keeps the how fluid and alive. Susan Zappo, the founder of Marriage Restoration, says it succinctly and truly: "One spouse with the help of God can save a marriage." Without that sense of mystery and destiny, it is difficult to sustain a marriage, especially in times of trouble. There is something about that sense of purpose that makes it seem safe and possible to reconcile with love and joy.

The process I have called heartstorming can be applied to any obstacle on the road of life. Heartstorming works because it is more than a technique to fix the broken parts of life. It works because its steps are based on the natural flow from heart to mind to soul and back again. It's the way we function: from heart to mind to soul. Even when, for whatever reason, the heart has been suppressed, that very suppression influences how the mind processes life. There is a dim frustration or a colorlessness about the contents of the mind. All of us have known people we perceived as cold and unfeeling. They tend to see life in terms of "strict justice" and as "matter of fact." The irony is that in such people (at one point in my life, I was one of them) the heart and the soul are still working, though at a much-diminished level. The heart, neglected and discouraged, feeds coldness to the mind, and receives it in return. The soul, though not consulted for a sense of mystery or purpose, can still communicate to the mind a sense of safety and rightness, but in a distorted way. We see it in people who, for example, need to be right at all costs—their righteousness is a harbor of safety in the face of the unpredictability of life.

With heartstorming, we take the parentheses off the heart and allow its impressions—however joyless, however sad—to touch the mind and to question its certainties and to help it discover new truths about life and new vistas of living. Then, we take away the parentheses we have placed around the mind and around the soul and allow them to be touched in a new way, with a lively sense of truth and of mystery. No longer do we see the unpredictability of life as an enemy against which we must close down our hearts and steel our minds. Instead, we come to see that the random events of life—even the tragic ones—actually move us closer to our reason for being here: touching hearts to make the world a better place.

Heartstorming is an important process, because the tragic events of life don't just go away the first time they happen. I mentioned previously the succession of losses of dear friends that occurred as I was writing this book. I want to say a little more about two of them: my cat, Flicka, and my very close friend, Ned Giordano. They deserve a special mention both because of who they were in my life and because I want to emphasize how important and helpful the heartstorming process is as we learn to treasure our departed ones.

Looking back, I think Flicka had been preparing us for her death for several months. Though she and Teddy had long been a couple, she began to distance herself from him and even appeared to disdain his company. She knew, I think, that unless she did that, Teddy would be too heartbroken to go on when the time came. Three days before she died, she hopped up and pulled a steak from my plate and devoured it before my eyes! I think she wanted to leave that funny memory for me as part of her legacy. On Wednesday night, she ate her dinner and went off quietly by herself. The next morning, she was dead. She died just as she had lived, completely on her own terms.

Ned Giordano was the dearest friend anyone could have. When he died, a day after Flicka, I thought my heart would break in two. When I spoke to his wife Linda, whom he adored, we recalled that Ned, a man of deep religious conviction, had often expressed the belief that one dies when it is time. "We are here on earth for a short time," he would say, "and then we go to heaven." Ned's conviction about that touched Linda's soul and mine and helped us to see his death not as a cruel, random event, but as part of the mystery of life—the way Ned saw it. That is what heartstorming can do. Our hearts were still broken, but that soul truth massaged our minds and hearts and helped us to go on.

With heartstorming, we see life steadily and see it whole. Whenever Ned and I met, upon departing he would always say to me, "Go safe." Heartstorming enables us to do just that—to go safe, knowing that as we encounter the storms of life, we are in the hands of God.

After he created the world and all the various creatures in it, God created man and woman. When that was done, he turned them loose to explore the world that he had made. The world was a vast place, and God was concerned that his creatures might get lost. So he endowed their nature with three gifts that would always allow him to find them no matter where they were.

With the *heart* God gave his creatures feelings that would always enable him to know if they were happy or well or ecstatic or in danger or concerned about something. When he heard the messages coming from their hearts, God sent them gifts from his own heart to address their needs—courage, approbation, guidance, inspiration. Wherever his creatures were, God could find them by tuning in to their hearts and guiding them.

With the *mind* God gave his creatures the ability to be curious, to question and to learn. Whenever his mind picked up on one of their questions, God sent them, in return, the understanding that they needed to resolve their dilemma. Wherever his creatures were, God could find them by tuning in to their minds and teaching them.

With the *soul* God gave his creatures the ability to see life whole, and to revere it. Whenever his soul picked up on their desire to put things into perspective so as to contribute to the good of the world, God sent them, in return, the warm, endearing power of his love so that they would always be safe, know that they were loved, and be aware that nothing was without its reason. Wherever his creatures were, God could find them by tuning in to their souls and loving them.

One day, God realized that something was terribly wrong. His heart could not feel the hearts of his creatures—there was nothing there. His mind could not tell what they needed to know—it was blank. His soul could not tell if they were safe—there was no signal from their souls. God was heartsick—he had lost his creatures, his loved ones. He had to find them.

Eons later, God is still looking for us, just as truly as we are looking for God. Remember that, when you probe the feelings of your heart to try to discern the waves and storms you often find there. When you use your mind to understand the puzzles of life, remember that in those puzzles, God is searching for the truth about you, just as you are searching for the truth in what you feel. When you soulfully seek purpose and ultimate meaning in and beyond the truths of your life—when you seek to believe that it is safe to be fully alive, recall that God has made it his purpose to find you—and, when you are found, to love you more than you know.

God has made it his business to heartstorm for you just as you make it your business to heartstorm for ultimate safety and for ultimate purpose in your life.

As Martin Luther said, "The human heart is like a ship on a stormy sea driven about by winds blowing from all four corners of heaven." Learning heartstorming, we learn to listen to those winds. They may often be frightening, ominous sounds. But as we tune in to our hearts, our minds, and our souls, we listen again to those gales. No longer are they just heartstorms that we hear. They are the voice of God, desperate to find us.

Suggested Reading

Abiven, Jean. *15 Days of Prayer with Saint Teresa of Avila*. Liguori, MO: Liguori Publications, 2000.

Cotner, June. *Bless the Day: Prayers and Poems to Nurture Your Soul*. New York: Kodansha International, 1998.

Dyer, Wayne. *Wisdom of the Ages: 60 Days to Enlightenment*. New York: HarperCollins, 1998.

St. John of the Cross. *The Collected Works of St. John of the Cross*. Translated by Kieran Kavanaugh and Otilio Rodriguez. Washington, DC: ICS Publications, 1979.

Keating, Thomas. *Active Meditations for Contemplative Prayer*. New York: Continuum Publishing Group, 1997.

Leshan, Lawrence. *How to Meditate: A Guide to Self-Discovery*. Boston: Little, Brown & Co., 1999.

Merton, Thomas. *The Seven Storey Mountain*. San Diego: Harcourt, 1999.

Straus, Celia. *More Prayers on My Pillow*. New York: Ballantine Books, 2000.

St. Teresa of Avila. *Interior Castle*. New York: Image Books, 1972.

St. Therese of Lisieux. *The Autobiography of Saint Therese of Lisieux: The Story of a Soul*. New York: Image Books, 1987.

Literary Credits

Index

317